MANCHESTER TO LIVERPOOL

via the Cheshire Lines
including the WIDNES CENTRAL Loop

Adrian Hartless

Front cover: Trafford Park Junction was one of the busiest points on the CLC main line. On 29th June 1965 our photographer recorded two steam trains there simultaneously. Fairburn 4MT 2-6-4T no. 42113 was working a rush hour local passenger service, probably the 18.05 Manchester Central – Irlam. It passed BR Standard 4MT 4-6-0 no. 75043 waiting at the end of the goods line from Throstle Nest South Junction with a freight; this loco was allocated to Aintree and so the train was likely heading for the North Liverpool line. No. 42113, a Trafford Park resident since November 1960, had but a short time to run, being withdrawn during the week ending 24th July following, but the unkempt Standard lingered on until the end of 1967.

Trafford Park Junction, later Trafford Park West Junction, was at the rear of the passenger train; the three-doll shunting signal at the extreme left indicated the course of the line into the goods yard and loco shed. The building behind the signals was the South Stand of Manchester United FC, and the platform serving the stadium was visible immediately beyond the junction. Trafford Park Junction signal box stood on the down side, obscured by the passenger train. The CLC footbridge was subsequently replaced by a much wider structure more suited to match day crowds. (T. Heavyside)

Back cover: Railway Clearing House map (edited), dated 1947. The route of the album is shown with a dotted line.

ACKNOWLEDGEMENTS

This book is dedicated to my old hometown friend Barry Allsopp (1938-2023) who spent much of his working life on the railway. We travelled together extensively including visits to the CLC main line and he crept into at least one picture in this volume.

I also want to remember Michael Payne (1950-2022) who was a son of Salford and a close neighbour. He will be remembered most as a solicitor and judge in Oxford for nearly 40 years but, like many of our generation, he was a schoolboy trainspotter who never lost his interest in railways.

Much gratitude goes to Jill for her sterling support of my contributions to the Middleton Press project of chronicling the wonderful world of our railways!

Additionally, I am grateful for the assistance received from many of those mentioned in the credits, particularly Doug Birmingham, and also Godfrey Croughton, Geoff Gartside, Chris Howard, Norman Langridge, Brian Read, David and Dr Susan Salter and Michael Stewart.

Published July 2024

ISBN 978 1 910356 88 3
© Middleton Press Ltd, 2024

Cover design and Photographic enhancement
  Deborah Esher
Production Cassandra Morgan

Published by
  Middleton Press Ltd
  Camelsdale Road
  Haslemere
  Surrey
  GU27 3RJ
Tel: 01730 813169
Email: info@middletonpress.co.uk
www.middletonpress.co.uk

Printed and bound by CPI Group (UK) Ltd,
  Croydon, CR0 4YY

Abbreviations:
CLC - Cheshire Lines Committee
FLT - Freightliner Terminal
GC - Great Central Railway
G&L - Garston & Liverpool Railway
GN - Great Northern Railway
L&Y - Lancashire & Yorkshire Railway
LCS - Liverpool Central Station and Railway
LMR - London Midland Region of British Railways
LMS - London, Midland & Scottish Railway
LNE - London & North Eastern Railway
LNW - London & North Western Railway
LOR - Liverpool Overhead Railway
MS&L - Manchester, Sheffield & Lincolnshire Railway
MSC - Manchester Ship Canal Company
MSD - Manchester South District Railway
MSJ&A - Manchester South Jn & Altrincham Railway
ROC - Rail Operating Centre
ROF - Royal Ordnance Factory
SH&RG - St Helens & Runcorn Gap Railway
SHCR - St Helens Canal & Railway Company
ST&A - Stockport, Timperley & Altrincham Railway
TOPS - Total Operations Processing System
TPE - TransPennine Express

SECTIONS

1. Manchester Oxford Road to Liverpool Central   1-114
2. Widnes Central Loop   115-120

CONTENTS

95	Aigburth	73	Halewood	107	St James
	(form. Mersey Road)	70	Hough Green	98	St Michael's
50	Birchwood	79	Hunts Cross	65	Sankey for Penketh
101	Brunswick	29	Humphrey Park	115	Tanhouse Lane
33	Chassen Road	41	Irlam	28	Trafford Park
12	Cornbrook	108	Liverpool Central	30	Urmston
93	Cressington	87	Liverpool South Parkway	58	Warrington Central
6	Deansgate	1	Manchester Oxford Road	63	Warrington West
	(form. Knott Mill)	16	Manchester United Halt	67	Widnes
34	Flixton	97	Otterspool		(form. Farnworth/
88	Garston	52	Padgate		Widnes North)
46	Glazebrook	49	ROF Risley	119	Widnes Central

Note: Manchester Central does not feature in this volume, having already appeared in *Chester Northgate to Manchester*. It will be covered again in a future volume that will include the former Midland Railway route from Cheadle Heath.

I. The Railway Clearing House map (edited) of 1947 has the route of this album in dark grey.

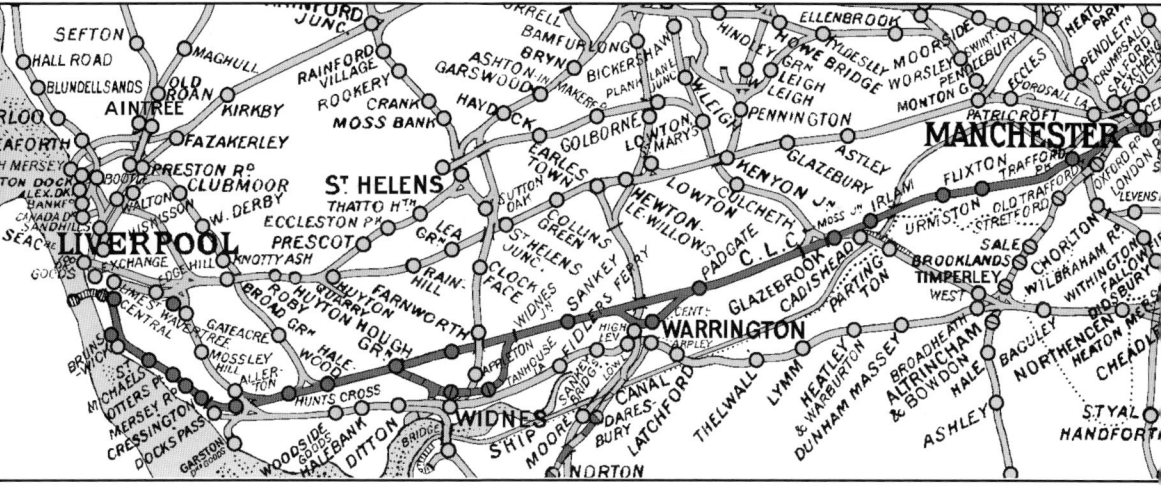

II. Our route from east to west is in the down direction of travel.

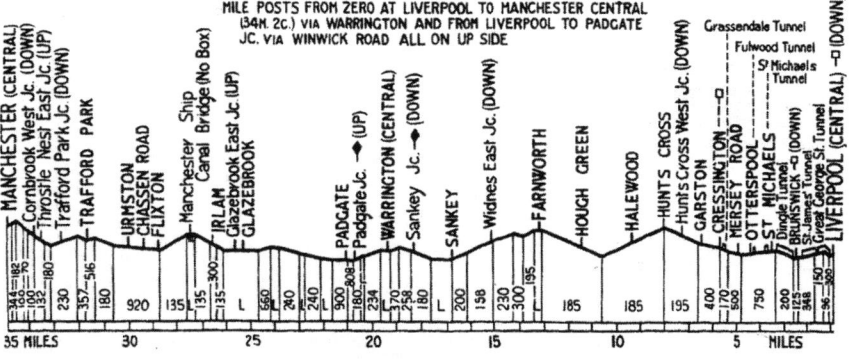

GEOGRAPHICAL SETTING

Manchester is located in the lower valley of the River Irwell which joins the Mersey near Irlam. Beyond this our route, mostly straight and easily graded, crosses the southern part of Chat Moss before reaching Warrington, for many years the lowest bridging point across the Mersey. The line continues broadly parallel with and north of the Mersey estuary until coming within half a mile of the foreshore at Cressington. It then turns northwest, still parallel with the estuary and a ridge of sandstone encroaches on its eastern side through which several tunnels were required to reach the centre of Liverpool. The distance from Manchester Oxford Road to Liverpool Central is approximately 34¼ miles.

All maps in the album are derived from 25ins to 1 mile editions dated 1925-37 with north at the top, unless otherwise indicated.

HISTORICAL BACKGROUND

The first 1¼ miles of our route, from Manchester Oxford Road to Cornbrook Junction, were opened on 20th July 1849 by the Manchester South Junction & Altrincham Railway (MSJ&A), a joint venture of the London & North Western (LNW) and the Manchester, Sheffield & Lincolnshire Railways (MS&L).

The term Cheshire Lines was first used in the Great Northern (Cheshire Lines) Act of 13th July 1863 under which the Great Northern (GN) and the MS&L agreed to subscribe equally to the following lines: Cheshire Midland (Altrincham–Northwich), opened 1862-63; Stockport & Woodley, opened 1863; Stockport, Timperley & Altrincham (ST&A), opened 1865; and West Cheshire (Northwich–Helsby), opened 1869. The Cheshire Lines Transfer Act of 5th July 1865 authorised inter alia the construction of a 28-mile line from Old Trafford (amended to Cornbrook in the following year) to Cressington, on the Garston & Liverpool (G&L), another Cheshire Lines concern which had opened on 1st June 1864. It also admitted the Midland Railway to the partnership on equal terms, creating a tripartite joint railway that ultimately owned 143 route miles, the largest jointly owned railway network in the UK. The Cheshire Lines Committee (CLC) itself was formally constituted in 1866.

The CLC, guided by the ambition of Sir Edward Watkin, Chairman of the MS&L, embarked on a significant period of expansion. Its new city to city line provided competition with the Liverpool & Manchester Railway of 1830, by now part of the LNW, which ran further north via Newton-le-Willows. The first part of the CLC route to open, on 1st March 1873, was from Skelton Junction, on the ST&A, to Cressington. The main line was completed by the section from Cornbrook Junction to Glazebrook on 2nd September 1873. Grandly designed termini followed, Liverpool Central opening on 1st March 1874 and Manchester Central on 1st July 1880 (replacing temporary facilities provided from 9th July 1877). The primary aim of this new route between the two great cities of the northwest was to give the partners their own line to Liverpool thereby breaking the duopoly of the LNW and Lancashire & Yorkshire (L&Y). It quickly proved itself popular with customers on account of its regular, frequent and punctual service.

Branches from the CLC main line were:
- The Hunts Cross Chord from Allerton LNW, which opened on 14th May 1873 to provide access to the CLC goods depot at Wavertree & Edge Hill inherited from the G&L;
- To Widnes, opened from Widnes East Junction, midway between Sankey and Farnworth, on 3rd April 1877 as an MS&L/Midland joint venture and extended west to Hough Green to form the Widnes Central loop in 1879;
- The North Liverpool line from Halewood/Hunts Cross to Huskisson and Aintree Central, opened by the CLC on 1st December 1879 to access the North Liverpool docks and extended to Southport in 1884;
- Glazebrook to Wigan, opened throughout by the MS&L in 1884;
- Also, on 11th January 1892, Liverpool Central was enhanced by the two-platform terminus of the Mersey Railway which was built beneath the CLC terminus and provided links to the Wirral railways at Birkenhead and Rock Ferry via the Mersey Rail Tunnel.

The CLC throughout its existence hired in all its locomotives from the MS&L/GC/LNE but owned its own rolling stock. At the Grouping on 1st January 1923 it retained its independence since no-one could decide whether it should fall into either the London, Midland & Scottish (LMS) or London & North Eastern (LNE) groups. It finally ceased when the railways were nationalised from 1st January 1948 when it became part of the London Midland Region (LMR) of British Railways. But even in 2024 the rump of the main line had the Engineer's Line Reference 'Manchester, Castlefield Junction to Hunts Cross West Junction (CLC Line)'.

The first significant casualty of the routes in this volume was the Widnes Central loop which closed entirely in late 1964. Most of the services using Liverpool Central (main line) were transferred to Lime Street from 5th September 1966 using the Hunts Cross Chord. Manchester Central closed from 5th May 1969 when services were diverted to Oxford Road; the building subsequently became an exhibition and conference centre.

Liverpool Central (main line) closed from 17th April 1972 and was demolished. The CLC main line was closed to passenger trains thence to Hunts Cross, and goods traffic ended soon after. Happily the route was retained and incorporated into the Merseyrail 750V third rail network with services from Southport beneath Liverpool city centre to Garston commencing from the start of 1978 and extended to Hunts Cross in 1983. It thus became the only section of the CLC main line to date to have been electrified for passenger use.

Passenger numbers have increased since the Beeching cuts. New stations have opened at Humphrey Park, at Birchwood, and at Brunswick; a new station at Warrington West effectively replaced Sankey for Penketh, and Halewood re-opened at a new location 37 years after the first station closed. Liverpool South Parkway, an interchange with the Liverpool – Runcorn line, replaced Garston. And funding has been secured to re-open Liverpool St James which closed at the end of 1916.

Whilst in 2024 it was no longer possible to travel from Manchester Central to Liverpool Central, one could still journey from Manchester Oxford Road, a short walk from the former, to the low level station at Liverpool Central, with a change of train at Hunts Cross – but not as quickly as under the ownership of the CLC.

PASSENGER SERVICES
1898

These timetable extracts reflect the CLC passenger services at their zenith. Five tables were required to cover all the services using the line between Manchester Central and Liverpool Central or parts thereof.

Manchester – Warrington – Garston – Liverpool

By this time, 25 years after opening, the CLC route between Lancashire's two greatest cities was well established. This was one of the first railways in the world to introduce repeating interval or clock-face timetables. There was an hourly express departing at 30 minutes past each hour in both directions between 8.30am and 8.30pm (plus 9.30pm from Liverpool), Mondays to Saturdays. These all called at Warrington Central and were allowed 45 minutes, except for the 3.30pm up which ran non-stop via the Warrington Straight Line in 40 minutes. The only all stations services were the 7.10am from Liverpool which took the direct route via Farnworth and the 7.20am from Manchester which served the Widnes Central loop. The latter had 13 up trains and 17 down scheduled Monday-Friday.

Manchester – Glazebrook

The second extract (overleaf) shows separately the suburban service between Manchester and Glazebrook. Trains terminated variously at Urmston, Flixton, Irlam, Wigan, Warrington, Southport and Liverpool. Urmston had 32 departures to Manchester Central Monday-Friday.

Hunts Cross – Garston – Liverpool

The third extract, below, shows separately the suburban service between Hunts Cross and Liverpool, which was even more intensive with trains originating from Manchester, Stockport, Warrington, Widnes, Garston, Gateacre, Walton-on-the-Hill and Southport. Garston had 40 departures to Liverpool Central Monday-Friday.

Manchester – Warrington – Southport

Through CLC services between Manchester Central and Southport Lord Street used our route as far as Halewood before turning onto the North Liverpool line. There were 10 such trains Monday to Friday, including the 5.10pm club train which completed the journey in 60 minutes.

Godley – Stockport – West Timperley – Warrington – Garston – Liverpool

Trains on this route joined the CLC main line at Glazebrook East Junction and included through services to Liverpool Central from the Midland and GN systems.

There were five Midland day trains from London St Pancras departing at 10.5am, 12.10, 2.0, 4.0 and 5.0pm. These took between 5 hours 15 minutes and 5 hours and 45 minutes. (This compared with 4 hours 15 minutes by the fastest LNW services between London Euston and Liverpool Lime Street.) The 2.0pm ran via Manchester Central where the Liverpool coaches were attached to the 6.30pm CLC express.

There were also Midland trains from elsewhere: the 8.45am from Leicester, which combined with the 9.10am from Nottingham at Ambergate, to Manchester Central where through coaches for Liverpool were attached to the 11.30am CLC express; the 10.25am from Derby; and the 4.0pm from Derby which included through carriages from Bristol (dep. 12.35pm) and Nottingham (dep. 3.30pm via Ambergate). Trains not serving Manchester Central joined the CLC at Bredbury Junction, east of Stockport Tiviot Dale on the Stockport & Woodley line.

Great Northern services all originated from London King's Cross and ran via Retford and Sheffield Victoria, thence via Woodhead to Godley Junction where they took the Stockport & Woodley line, or via the Fallowfield loop to Manchester Central where through coaches for Liverpool were attached to CLC expresses. There were seven departures conveying through carriages from King's Cross between 5.15am and 5.30pm of which the fastest was the 2.0pm which reached Liverpool Central at 7.5pm.

Other pre-World War I services

On 15th March 1899 the MS&L opened its London Extension from Nottingham to London Marylebone and renamed itself the Great Central (GC) Railway. The ripples were felt as far away as the CLC main line. Whilst the GC did not attempt to gatecrash the already crowded daytime London to Liverpool market it did offer a through carriage on the night mail and newspaper services, 10.0pm ex Marylebone (arr. Liverpool Central 5.5am) and 9.30pm ex Liverpool (attached to the 10.20pm Manchester Central to Marylebone arr. 3.40am). There were also through carriages from Liverpool Central at 8.30am attached to the 9.20am Manchester Central to Bournemouth West (arr. 4.52pm) via Sheffield Victoria, Woodford & Hinton and Oxford.

The 1903 timetable also showed three through trains from Liverpool Central to Hull Paragon at 11.20am, 1.0pm and 4.5pm, which took a little over four hours. The Continental Boat Express left Liverpool Central at 1.33pm and had portions for Grimsby Docks (arr. 6.20pm) for daily sailings to Hamburg, and Harwich Parkeston Quay (arr. 9.30pm) for Hook of Holland. These all ran via Stockport Tiviot Dale. In the years preceding WW1 the balancing workings conveyed thousands of migrants from Northern Europe to Liverpool en route to the USA.

Post World War I

Whilst the CLC retained its independence under the 1923 railway grouping neither of its shareholders regarded it as a high priority for investment, and services generally stagnated. The only notable changes to the CLC expresses were the addition of a second intermediate stop, Farnworth, in 1930, and new rolling stock in 1937. The number of through services over the main line dwindled, for example, through carriages from King's Cross, and the trains became more local in nature.

1961

The timetable extracts below and overleaf are from the summer 1961 schedule for up services between Liverpool Central and Manchester Central. CLC services went over from steam to diesel units from the summer 1960 timetable. However there was no immediate attempt to improve on the time-honoured 45 minute express schedule between the two cities. Departures both ways were still hourly at xx.30. Stopping services ran generally hourly from Liverpool Central, to Warrington at xx.12 and to Gateacre at xx.42. They were less frequent from Manchester Central outside the peak hours. After the 9.33am to Warrington there was a three-hour gap Monday-Friday until the 12.33pm to Wigan Central. This preceded five down departures up to the 1.35pm to Warrington. There were then only two further locals until the evening peak began after 4.30pm. Off peak services on the Widnes Central loop had ceased entirely.

The only surviving long-distance trains from Liverpool Central all ran via Manchester Central and comprised through carriages for Hull attached to the 9.30am up express, the 1.15pm to Harwich (successor to the Continental Boat Express), the 4.52pm to Hull, and through coaches coupled to the 9.30pm up express for the overnight journey to London Marylebone; the latter was withdrawn soon after as part of the run-down to closure of the former Great Central London Extension.

1969-86

As noted above, the 1960s saw the closure of the Widnes Central loop (and also the Wigan Central branch), and both Liverpool Central and Manchester Central stations. From 5th May 1969 CLC main line trains ran from Manchester Piccadilly and/or Oxford Road to Liverpool Lime Street. The summer 1983 timetable was typical of this period with 12 express services in the up direction, starting at 08.35 and then hourly from 09.29, taking generally 50 minutes to Piccadilly. Down expresses mostly departed Piccadilly at xx.27. The off-peak slow service consisted of an all-stations train at xx.09 from Lime Street to Warrington (arr. xx.49) which returned after a 21 minute layover, and at xx.07 from Oxford Road to Warrington (arr. xx.43) which returned at xx.12. Both provided connections into and out of the expresses at Warrington.

1986

From 12th May 1986 the Hazel Grove Chord was brought into use. This allowed the hourly fast services between Sheffield and Manchester, which hitherto used the former Midland Railway Hope Valley line thence the suburban approach to Manchester Piccadilly via New Mills Central, to join the ex-LNW Buxton branch at Hazel Grove instead and so reach Piccadilly via Stockport Edgeley. They all used the MSJ&A through platform at Piccadilly before continuing to Liverpool Lime Street via the CLC route. This longer distance service re-introduced locomotive haulage on the CLC until the introduction of new diesel units from around 1990.

Clock-face scheduling was perpetuated with a departure at 45 minutes past the hour from Liverpool from 08.45 until 19.45, plus 21.45. These were generally timed to reach Manchester Oxford Road in 48 minutes inclusive of stops at Warrington Central and Birchwood. All these trains continued beyond Manchester, terminating variously at Sheffield (5 services), Hull (5), Cleethorpes (2), and Yarmouth (1). The down timetable was similar with hourly fast services leaving Piccadilly at 20 minutes past the hour and mostly scheduled to reach Lime Street in 47 minutes with the same two stops.

The other CLC stations were well-served by an hourly all stops service between Hunts Cross and Manchester Oxford Road with departures from 07.04 until 23.04, generally taking 64 minutes including 14 intermediate stops. There was a handful of Monday-Friday peak hour extras. Hunts Cross to Liverpool Central was served by Merseyrail every 15 minutes between 07.06 and 19.06, and otherwise every 30 minutes between 06.06 and 23.36, taking 14 minutes including four intermediate stops.

2006

The 2006 timetable may be used to illustrate the impact of privatisation on the CLC main line which had four Train Operating Companies, at this time Central, Northern, TransPennine Express (TPE), and Merseyrail west of Hunts Cross. Central ran hourly from Liverpool to Norwich, via Sheffield, Nottingham and Peterborough, a distance of 252 miles, nine times daily with a further five trips to Nottingham and one to Cambridge. TransPennine ran hourly to Scarborough via Huddersfield and Leeds. This gave the CLC main line two expresses per hour, evenly spaced, for example, leaving Liverpool Lime Street at xx.22 and xx.52. The Central service was allowed 46 minutes to Oxford Road including stops at Widnes and Warrington and the TransPennines were booked to take 44 minutes with calls at Warrington and Birchwood. Northern contributed two hourly stopping services between Lime Street and Oxford Road taking 66-70 minutes and serving all stations at least once every hour except for Glazebrook, Chassen Road, Humphrey Park and Trafford Park which were every two hours off-peak. Certain services in both directions terminated at Warrington, especially in the evenings. The Merseyrail service pattern continued with little change; the schedule to Liverpool Central had been eased to 17 minutes following the opening of Brunswick. At this time there was no Sunday service at Trafford Park, Humphrey Park, Chassen Road, Flixton, Irlam, Glazebrook, Padgate, and Sankey for Penketh.

2023

The post-pandemic timetable was not dissimilar to that of 2006. Off-peak the CLC saw four trains per hour. TPE now ran to Cleethorpes, at xx.19 from Liverpool Lime Street reaching Manchester Oxford Road in 48 minutes with stops at Liverpool South Parkway, Warrington Central, Birchwood, Irlam and Urmston. East Midlands Railway perpetuated the Norwich route with xx.51 departures serving Liverpool South Parkway, Widnes and Warrington Central and taking 46 minutes. Northern ran two trains hourly. The first was xx.22 Lime Street–Oxford Road, calling at all stops to Liverpool South Parkway, then Hough Green and Warrington West before Warrington Central; from there all trains stopped at Padgate, Birchwood, Irlam, Flixton and Urmston, whilst every other service called at either Glazebrook and Chassen Road or Humphrey Park and Trafford Park. Scheduled journey time was 71 minutes including 14 stops. The second was xx.56 Lime Street – Warrington Central serving all stops except Edge Hill and Sankey for Penketh, whose only calls were one each way in both the morning and evening peaks following the opening of Warrington West.

Future Plans

On 4th October 2023 the UK Government announced the cancellation of the second phase of HS2, Birmingham – Manchester, citing spiralling costs. The funds released would be re-directed to other transport projects, including Northern Powerhouse Rail. Whether this would have a significant impact on the CLC route, for example, electrification, was not specified.

1. Manchester Oxford Road to Liverpool Central

MANCHESTER OXFORD ROAD

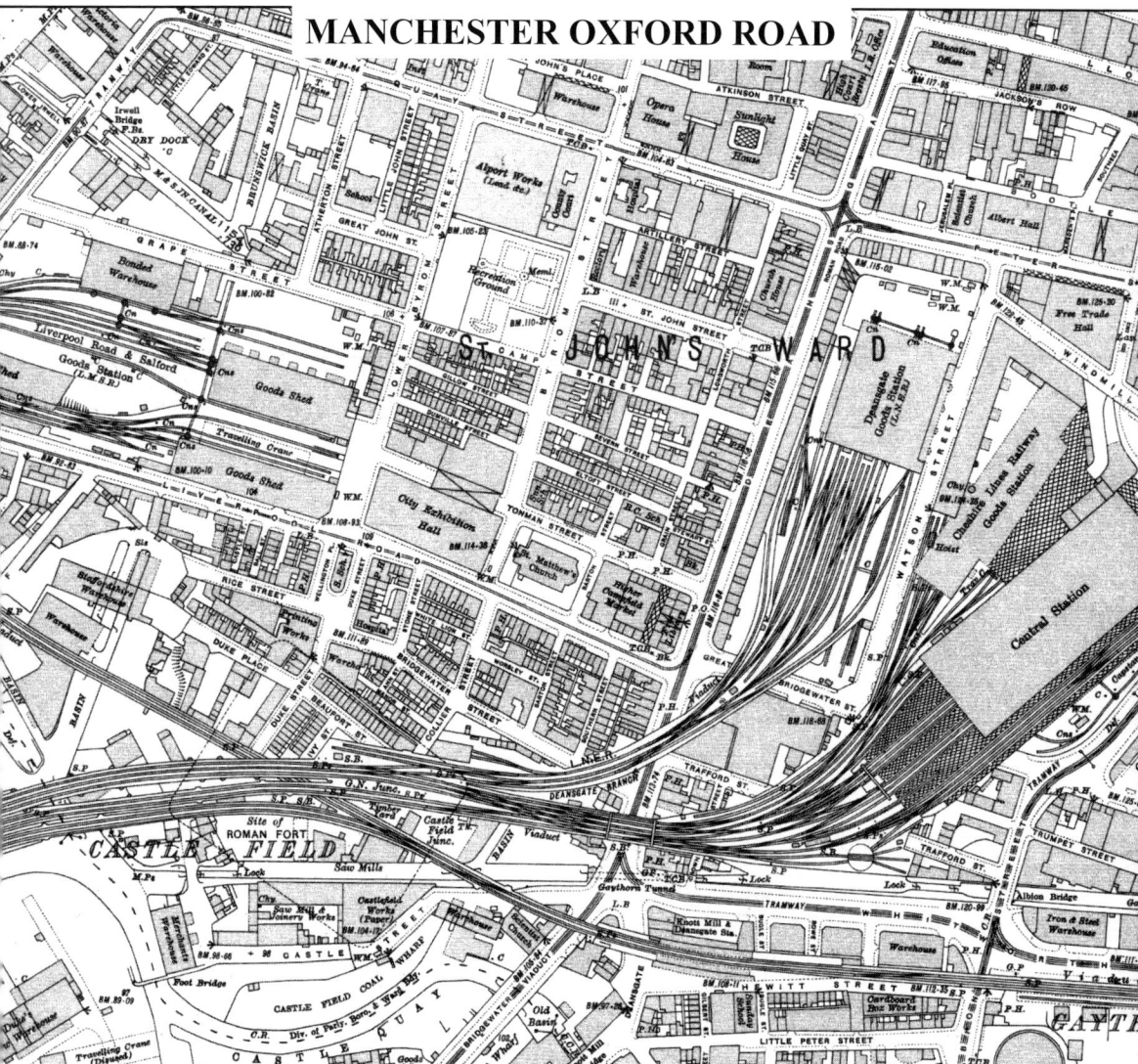

III. The map is from 1932 and highlights the proximity of Manchester Central. Oxford Road station (bottom right) underwent many changes subsequently although its layout was still identifiable. Oxford Road itself was traditionally the main road south from Manchester, commencing at St Peter's Square. It was incorporated as the Manchester – Wilmslow Turnpike in 1753, the most northerly section of the route to Oxford, later the A34. Since the late 19th century that part of the road within the boundary of the city centre was called Oxford Street.

The station opened with the Altrincham line on 20th July 1849 as a southwest-facing two platform terminus at the corner of Oxford Road and Whitworth Street West. Just 12 days later the Manchester South Junction line opened between London Road and Ordsall Lane, linking the routes from Manchester to Crewe and to Sheffield with the former Liverpool & Manchester Railway, and a bi-directional through platform was added creating the V-shaped footprint that was still evident in 2024.

Despite considerable traffic growth a second through platform was not provided until 1903. This is the state of play shown on the map with a goods loop and two sidings south of the new platform. In 1931 the London Road – Altrincham line was electrified using 1500V DC overhead cables, including all four platforms at Oxford Road.

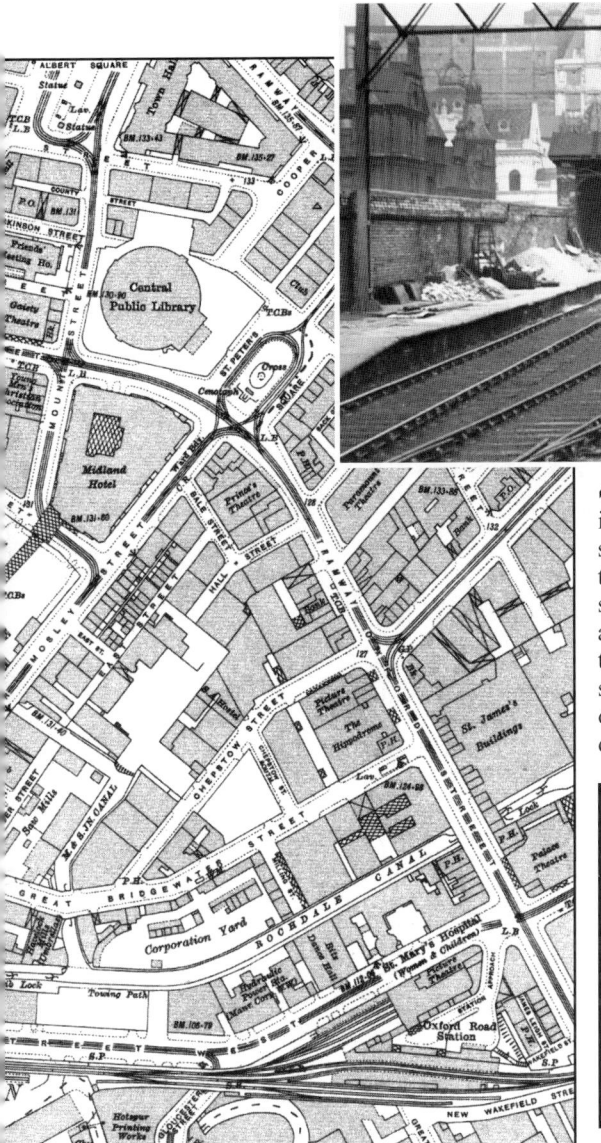

↑ 1. We start with the terminal platforms, seen in February 1948; note the carriage sidings which separated the two platform roads. There appeared to be building work in progress on the left-hand side. A train shed covered the two left hand roads, and there had been one also over the other two tracks, a victim of bomb damage in 1941. The two-storey building on the right formerly housed the offices of the MSJ&A. A three-car EMU awaited departure for Altrincham. (LGRP/R. Humm coll.)

> **Further pictures of Oxford Road can be seen in** *Chester Northgate to Manchester*. **Other pictures of the area can be found in the following albums:** *Manchester to Bacup*, *Crewe to Manchester (including the Styal Line)* **and** *Manchester & Ashton Trolleybuses.*

The next major developments were in 1958-60 when the station was completely rebuilt in connection with the Crewe – Manchester 25kV AC electrification. The new platform of 1903 was converted to an island, and the goods loop became the down through platform line. The former down through line was redesignated the up through line, whilst the former up through line, the single line of 1849, became an east-facing bay for local electric trains to and from Crewe. The two lines in the original terminus were retained, primarily for the Altrincham service, which was still wired at 1500V. Colour light signalling replaced semaphores.

This stage lasted only nine years. In 1969, following the closure of Manchester Central, a fourth through platform was built on the south side of the formation, and the more northerly of the two lines in the original terminus was lifted. The platforms were renumbered 1-5 from south to north. The MSJ&A DC electrification was replaced by 25kV AC from 3rd May 1971 when the track serving the original through platform was restored to a through line.

The range of destinations served from Oxford Road in 2023 would have baffled a time traveller from 1873. These included Norwich, Llandudno, Blackpool, Scarborough, Edinburgh, Glasgow, Southport and Manchester Airport – but not Altrincham whose route was transferred to Manchester Metrolink in 1992.

2. This splendid southwesterly view was obtained from the Refuge Assurance clock tower on 13th March 1959 and showed the station mid-way through the throes of rebuilding. The terminal lines were on the right, temporarily out of use whilst the work progressed. The carriage sidings had been abolished and most of the buildings seen in picture no. 1 had been flattened. The two through lines were on the left and an Altrincham EMU occupied the down line. New shelters had been constructed on three of the four platforms. At the bottom left was the timber-built two-storey building of 1903, which was the main entrance and booking office with further offices above and which was demolished soon afterwards, whilst in the centre of the view the framework of its successor was taking shape. At the end of the through platforms could be seen the 'back line' coming into view from behind the down side, also the two sidings, the further one of which held four open wagons. The two running lines could be followed along the viaduct out of the picture towards Knott Mill & Deansgate. (British Railways)

↗*(top)* 3. Looking somewhat anachronistic, Ivatt 2MT 2-6-2T no. 41211 worked a Warrington Bank Quay Low Level local via Broadheath at the northerly bay platform. This was a push-pull service, and the train appeared to be departing. The loco was allocated to 8B Warrington in April 1961 and the service was withdrawn from 10th September 1962, so the date of the picture most likely fell between the two. At left an AM4 (later class 304) EMU stood at the buffer stops, which marked the limit of the 25kV electrification from Crewe between 1960-69. The running-in board at left called the station Manchester Oxford Road, but the totems merely Oxford Road. The signal box was built in 1897 to a Great Central design. It closed on 20th April 1969 when control passed to Manchester London Road Power Signal Box (illustrated in *Crewe to Manchester*). This was replaced by Manchester Piccadilly PSB in 1988, and its functions were in turn transferred to the Manchester Rail Operating Centre (ROC), located at Ashburys, on 28th December 2016. (R.H. Hughes)

↗*(middle)* 4. This has been the prospective passenger's perspective since 1960, a bold conoid design, likened by some to an armadillo. Like its predecessor it was mostly made of wood, as were also the new platform shelters. It is of considerable architectural interest and was listed Grade II along with the other timber structures in 1995 after only 35 years use. It was seen on 26th May 2016; the windows reflected three cranes and the Refuge Assurance building. (A.C. Hartless)

→ 5. This was an eastward view on the same day from platform 1. At platform 2 was the 12.50 Scarborough – Liverpool TPE service via Newton-le-Willows formed of Desiro DMU no. 185136, whilst at platform 5 no. 156461 was ready to depart with the 15.16 Northern service to Liverpool via the CLC route. Signals could be seen at the far end of both platforms 1 and 2; all four through platforms were bi-directional. Peering over the footbridge was the clock tower that for many years bore the word REFUGE. Refuge Assurance decamped to Wilmslow in 1987 and the building subsequently became a hotel. (A.C. Hartless)

DEANSGATE

Map III (next to picture 1) locates the station towards the bottom middle of the left-hand page.

The MSJ&A ran westward along the southern edge of the City of Manchester, as it became on 29th March 1853, before it intersected Deansgate, just 28 chains from Oxford Road. The entire line from London Road (Piccadilly) to Knott Mill was built on arches, 130 in all. This has, to date, precluded widening the route from its two tracks, except through Oxford Road station. Often referred to as the Castlefield Corridor, it is one of the busiest two track lines in Britain with around 25 trains per hour at peak times.

The station provided here was initially known as Knot Mill. This was soon officially altered to Knott Mill. It is unclear when the suffix Deansgate was first used, unofficially quite early, officially by 1882. However, when the station was rebuilt in 1895-96, in brick instead of timber, the name affixed to the exterior was shown as KNOTT MILL STATION, which it still carried in 2024. It was officially renamed simply Deansgate from 3rd May 1971. The structures dating from 1896 were listed Grade II in 1998.

Deansgate itself is Manchester's main central thoroughfare running south from Victoria Street to cross the River Medlock south of the railway after which it turns southwest to become Chester Road. The station is close to the eastern end of the Bridgewater Canal (marked Old Basin on the map) which opened in 1761. There were only ever two platforms here, and no approach road, only steps up from the street until lifts were installed in 1989. A footbridge was constructed across Whitworth Street West in 1984 to link with the Greater Manchester Exhibition Centre (G-Mex), then under redevelopment from Manchester Central station. When Metrolink opened in 1992 G-Mex tram stop was located at the opposite end of the footbridge; it was renamed Deansgate-Castlefield from 20th September 2010.

6. An eastward view from autumn 1963 featured an MSJ&A EMU arriving en route from Oxford Road to Altrincham. The canopies were thought to date from 1945 following war damage. (D.L. Chatfield)

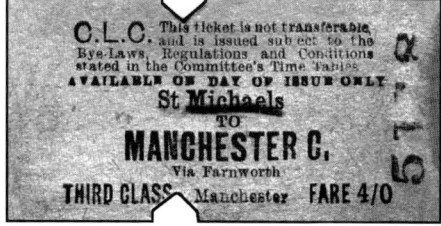

7. A westward view from 27th October 2000 showed DMU no. 156440 at platform 1 with the 09.54 Blackpool North – Manchester Airport. This had travelled from Bolton via the Windsor Link, which opened in 1988 between Salford Crescent and Ordsall Lane, whilst the Manchester Airport branch opened in 1993. The canopies had been renewed in 1989. (A.C. Hartless)

← 8A. On the same day the west-end entrance was recorded from the path adjacent to Metrolink (formerly the station throat of Manchester Central). The contemporary Deansgate name sign managed to complement the Knott Mill Station scroll of 1896. The vaguely castellated architectural style was a reference to the Roman fort at Castlefield from which Manchester derives its name, and which was largely obliterated by the MSJ&A. Lower Deansgate was bridged at right; this was by-passed in 1919 by Bridgewater Viaduct. (A.C. Hartless)

↓ 8B. A final picture from 27th October 2000 showed the northeast elevation of the station. At bottom left a light van was emerging from Bugle Street to join Whitworth Street West. The building behind it carried the branding REGIONAL RAILWAYS (which was in use between 1982-97 but had not yet been removed) although it was not part of the station. The ramped pedestrian access from the street dated from the 1896 improvements. Above it, at right, was the footbridge to Metrolink. (A.C. Hartless)

WEST OF DEANSGATE

At Castlefield Junction, 10 chains beyond Deansgate, the MSJ&A split into two lines, the South Junction continuing to Ordsall Lane, and the Altrincham line branching left. The latter closely followed the Bridgewater Canal, crossing its Castlefield Basin and continuing along the 47 chain Cornbrook Viaduct. Adjacent ran the parallel viaduct opened in 1877 to carry the CLC lines from Manchester Central, which bridged the South Junction line before gradually descending to the same height as the Altrincham line at Cornbrook.

↑ 9. On a date in circa 1967 an Oxford Road – Altrincham EMU was seen from Egerton Street on Cornbrook Viaduct. In the foreground was the Bridgewater Canal. Behind the train were the structures leading to Manchester Central, whose distinctive arched roof was in the upper right background. The girder bridge partly concealed by the crane jib carried the CLC over the South Junction line, and below its right-hand end was Castlefield Junction signal box, which closed from 20th April 1969. The five track CLC line closed from 5th May 1969 but two tracks were brought back into use by Metrolink from 15th June 1992. (J. Clark, courtesy Book Law Publications)

◤ 10. Looking the other way on 11th May 1990, Railfreight liveried no. 47095 rattled across Castlefield Junction with the 18.09 Trafford Park – Warrington Arpley Speedlink. Both the MSJ&A and the CLC viaducts could be seen stretching towards Cornbrook; the eagle-eyed might have spotted a class 303 EMU on a Crewe – Altrincham local on the former. It was approaching a section of the viaduct destroyed by the Luftwaffe in December 1941 and which took nine months to replace. (P.D. Shannon)

11. A view west from Deansgate on 27th October 2000 revealed Castlefield Junction in the middle distance. Pacer DMU no. 142056 had come off the South Junction line with the 10.28 Liverpool – Manchester Airport via Newton-le-Willows. It had passed beneath the former CLC viaduct that had just been crossed by a first generation Metrolink tram on an inbound service approaching the G-Mex stop. The South Junction line was electrified in 2013, 82 years after the Altrincham route. (A.C. Hartless)

CORNBROOK

There was an MSJ&A station at Cornbrook between 1856-65 serving the Pomona Pleasure Gardens, but no pictures are known. (Pomona was the Roman goddess of fruit trees, gardens and orchards.) The CLC route to Glazebrook opened on 2nd September 1873 from Cornbrook Junction, just to the south. This was renamed Cornbrook East Junction when the CLC line to Manchester Central opened, and its Chester and Liverpool services were redirected thence from Oxford Road. The point of divergence of the Manchester Central branch was named Cornbrook West Junction. It was further complicated when the Manchester Central route gained three further tracks and a second viaduct in 1898.

The area between the diverging Altrincham and Liverpool routes was used by the CLC for carriage sidings, including a 12-road shed, and a goods depot. The CLC also built a 3-road loco shed on a cramped site on the up side hard by the Bridgewater Canal, which was replaced by the much larger Trafford Park shed in 1895. One of the last uses of Cornbrook Sidings was to store the MSJ&A 1500V EMUs after their withdrawal in May 1971. The area was subsequently sold for redevelopment.

The Altrincham line closed south of Cornbrook East Junction on 24th December 1991 for conversion to Metrolink which utilised the formation of the two original CLC lines along the viaduct from G-Mex before passing beneath the Liverpool line to join the former MSJ&A near Trafford Bar. When the Eccles Metrolink line was opened in 2000 it joined the Altrincham line at Cornbrook where an interchange stop was provided adjacent to the site of the MSJ&A station.

12. This picture dates from circa 1893 and showed one of the Pomona Docks (probably no. 2) of the Manchester Ship Canal under construction. The building beyond was Cornbrook loco shed. The Bridgewater Canal ran between the two. The Pomona Docks fell into disuse after the mid-1960s and closed officially in 1982 with the rest of the Manchester Docks.
(P.H. Hanson coll.)

13. On 22nd October 2002 DMU no. 150145 passed Cornbrook Metrolink with the 14.27 Liverpool – Manchester Airport. It had joined the formation of the former MSJ&A line where the tracks curved right in the background at the site of Cornbrook East Junction. The low wall in the left foreground marked the start of the grade separation between the MSJ&A and CLC viaducts leading to the city centre. In the right background the Eccles Metrolink line branched left from the Altrincham line. The latter then descended to dive under the outbound Eccles and the CLC tracks. (A.C. Hartless)

SOUTHWEST FROM CORNBROOK

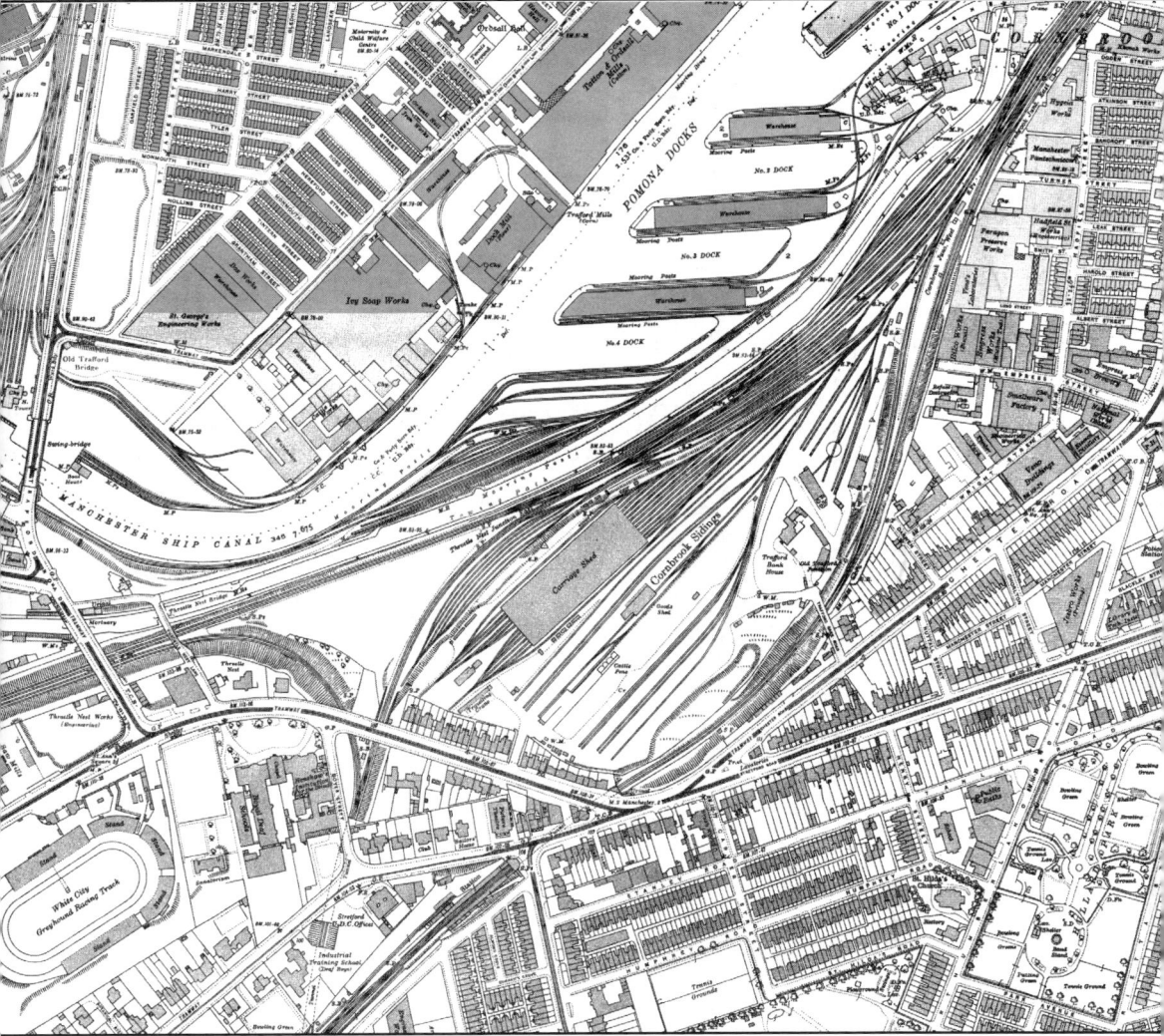

IV. As the CLC route came level with the carriage shed it reached Throstle Nest Junction. (Throstle Nest was the name of a nearby house which pre-dated both the Bridgewater Canal that used the name for a bridge, and the railway.) Here the Manchester South District (MSD) line of the Midland, opened 1st January 1880, branched off on the left initially to Stockport Tiviot Dale. This was the springboard for the Midland's main line from Manchester Central to London St Pancras. The CLC assumed responsibility for the MSD as far as Chorlton-cum-Hardy Junction in 1891 when the MS&L's Fallowfield loop line opened thence from Fairfield and Gorton. There was originally a tunnel of approximately 220 yards on the CLC immediately west of the Trafford Road bridge.

The CLC added a south to west curve at Throstle Nest in 1906 to facilitate goods services eastward from Trafford Park; these goods lines ran parallel to the main line for half a mile until Trafford Park Junction. The tunnel on the main line was opened out and Throstle Nest Junction was renamed Throstle Nest East Junction.

Throstle Nest East Junction to Throstle Nest South Junction closed with Manchester Central from 5th May 1969 along with the signal boxes at Cornbrook West Junction and Throstle Nest East Junction. Throstle Nest South Junction to Trafford Park Junction was last used on 15th October 1988. Cornbrook East Junction to Trafford Park Freightliner Terminal was electrified in 1980.

14. This splendid aerial view from 1954 could have been commissioned for this album. It traced our route, which leaves the frame at bottom left, from the Throstle Nest triangle back to Castlefield Junction. At the bottom of the picture a short goods train was making its way from Trafford Park towards Chorlton behind a J10 0-6-0 running tender first. Following the line of our route the signal box at Throstle Nest East Junction could be seen, backing onto the Bridgewater Canal. Across the tracks was Cornbrook Carriage Shed and its associated sidings, along with Cornbrook Goods; spot the turntable. Cornbrook Sidings signal box stood at the throat of the carriage sidings. The MSJ&A came in at the right margin, and as it converged with the CLC line Cornbrook West Junction signal box stood in the vee between the two routes, opposite which was the site of Cornbrook loco shed, evidenced by disused sidings. The two routes became parallel, the five-track CLC to the left and MSJ&A right, to cross the Cornbrook Viaducts. In the middle distance Castlefield Junction could be seen with the South Junction line coming in on the left from Ordsall Lane. Beyond that the Great Northern goods warehouse stood to the left of Central station (the left-hand section of whose roof could be discerned at the upper right margin), the two separated by the CLC goods station. There was much else to see. The Pomona Docks of the Port of Manchester were prominent, with the Ordsall district to their left. The line of the Liverpool & Manchester Railway ran left to right across the middle background before terminating at Liverpool Road whose elevated warehouses were visible. (Britain from the Air)

➔ 15. On 11th April 2014 no. 66707 *Sir Sam Fay* approached Trafford Road bridge with the 01.48 Felixstowe–Trafford Park. (Fay was General Manager of the GC from 1902-22.) To the right was the trackbed of the Throstle Nest South Junction – Trafford Park Junction goods lines. To the left was the Bridgewater Canal, and on its opposite bank the viaduct bearing the superstructure of Pomona Metrolink tramstop. At this time it served only the Eccles line, but in 2020 it became the junction for the new Trafford Centre branch. (P.D. Shannon)

MANCHESTER UNITED HALT

Manchester United FC relocated from Newton Heath in 1910 to a greenfield site at Old Trafford immediately north of the CLC route. It was not until 21st August 1935, however, that a single platform halt was opened for use on matchdays only, for which a loop from the up line was built. It was known variously as Manchester United Football Ground, Manchester United FC Halt, Old Trafford Halt and other permutations. This popular facility was last used on 10th December 2017, the opening day of the Ordsall Chord which brought further traffic to the Castlefield Corridor; but it is understood the football club requested the closure on Health & Safety grounds.

16. On 22nd September 1977 no. 40025 took the road into Trafford Park Yard with what looked like a partially brake-fitted goods, by then becoming an infrequent sight. The halt at left had five short flights of steps leading into the South Stand. In the background could be seen the end of the platform loop, followed beyond the bridge by Trafford Park East Junction giving access to the goods lines towards Chorlton-cum-Hardy. (T. Heavyside)

17. On 22nd August 2015 EMU no. 323228 stood at the halt after arrival with the 10.46 from Manchester Airport and would shortly return empty to Manchester. Behind the unit was Trafford Park West Junction leading to the Euroterminal. The Premier League match that day ended in a goalless draw with Newcastle. (P. Chandler)

EAST OF TRAFFORD PARK

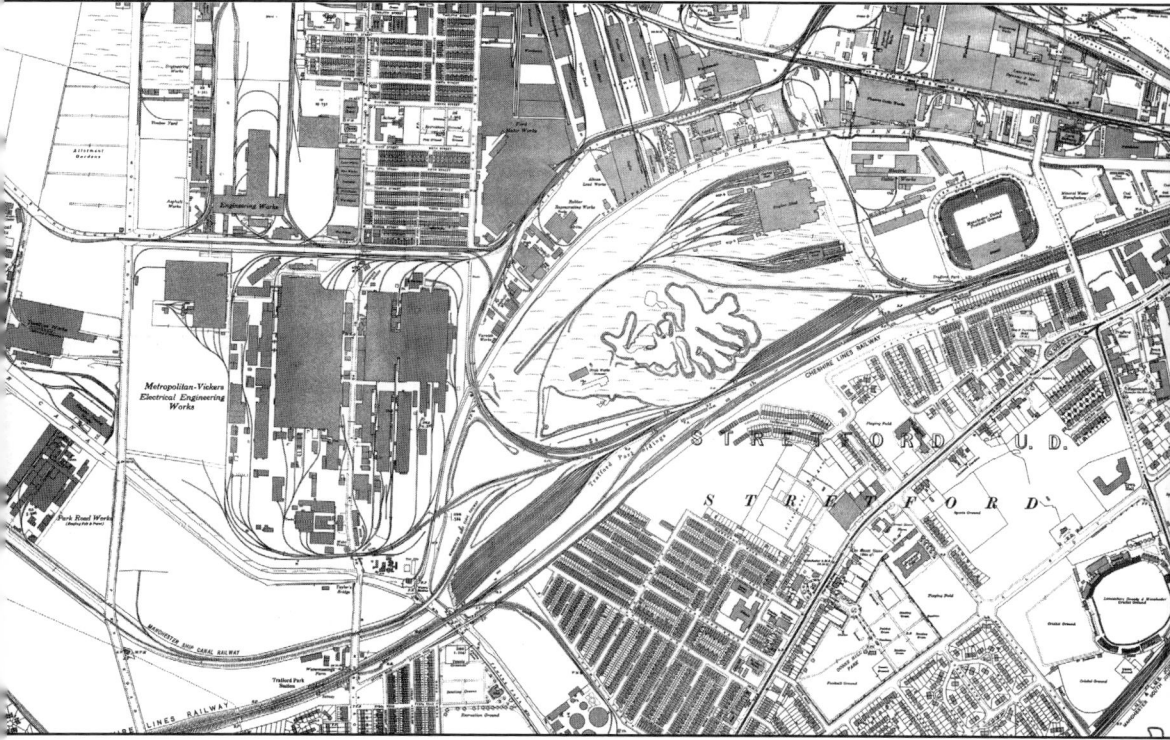

V. The original Trafford Park was the manor of the de Trafford family who came to England in 1016 with Canute and took their name from Treyford, a Roman crossing of the River Irwell nearby. Their ancestral home was Trafford Hall until the coming of the Ship Canal rendered it unsuitable for landed gentry. The house and grounds were sold in 1896 and the Trafford Park Industrial Estate, the first such enterprise in the world, began to be developed. Trafford Hall became a commercial hotel until it was demolished in 1926.

The CLC acquired land between its main line and the Bridgewater Canal in response to the opening of the Ship Canal and the start-up of the Industrial Estate for the purpose of sidings and Trafford Park loco shed, which opened in March 1895. The shed had no fewer than 20 roads which were split 50/50 between the CLC and the Midland. It was rarely worked to capacity and earned a reputation as a place where old locos were stored when not required, but it remained open until 6th May 1968 when steam ended in the Manchester area. At different times in LMS and BR days it was coded 13A, 17F, and 19G, but spent most of its time as 9E. It was accessed from Trafford Park West Junction and in 2024 the site was part of the Freightliner Terminal (FLT), used for storing shipping containers.

The sorting sidings occupied much of the land between the main line and the loco shed, handling traffic into and out of the Industrial Estate. This large site developed into Manchester's primary railfreight transhipment hub, which in 2024 comprised the FLT and the Euroterminal. It was one of the busiest inland railheads for intermodal traffic in the UK.

The Trafford Park Industrial Estate occupied a site of 4.75 square miles bounded by the Bridgewater and the Ship Canals. At its height it contained around 27 miles of railway sidings linked to the CLC by a bridge across the Bridgewater Canal. Shunting was performed by locomotives from the Manchester Ship Canal Company (MSC), and in 1970 the following businesses had their own internal shunters: Associated Electrical Industries Ltd, Victor Blagden Ltd, Redpath Dorman Long Ltd, Trafford Park Steel Works, Brown & Polson Ltd, Kraft Foods Ltd, Procter & Gamble Ltd, Shell-Mex/BP Ltd, Turners Asbestos Ltd and Edward Wood Ltd. The system was much reduced in the mid-1970s and last used in 2001.

Another branch, which opened in 1969, was an extension of the MSC Park Road Works line. It ran for 2 miles from the west end of the sorting sidings to the Barton Dock Estate to serve a new container terminal until rail traffic ceased in 2012.

18. This is a picture of the CLC side of the loco shed in around 1902. The locomotives were all clean, there was not a tile out of place on the roofs, and there was a commendable absence of waste ash or any other debris. This was par for the course pre-WWI. The roofing was symmetrical, three bays each covering three tracks, a central bay covering two, and three more of three. The locos on display were all from the Great Central fleet. Three were class 11A (LNER D6) 4-4-0s, nos 865, 866 and 874, from right to left. There were 33 of them, built between 1897-99 and they spent most of their lives on the CLC system; the last one was withdrawn at the end of 1947. The loco in the middle looked like a 9D (LNER J10) 0-6-0, and the one at far right appeared to be one of the six class 13 (LNER X4) 4-2-2s. Built in 1900 these were the last single wheelers on the GC; the last one was withdrawn in 1927. (R. Humm coll.)

19. This general view of 9E dates from 1952. All 20 roads were in view. In contrast with the previous view there was not a roof tile to be seen. A start had been made on re-roofing beginning with the most southerly bay on the right, corrugated steel replacing timber. The next four bays were subsequently treated similarly, but cut back in length, and the two most northerly bays were left open to air and used for a coal conveyor, which replaced the two coal stages shown on the map. Locomotives in view included a J10, two each of LMS Compound 4-4-0s and 4F 0-6-0s, and an LMS Hughes-Fowler 2-6-0. (LGRP/R. Humm coll.)

20. This view probably dates from late 1959. Fairburn 4MT 2-6-4T no. 42683 stood outside the most northerly of the surviving roof bays. To its left were two stored locomotives, Fowler 3MT 2-6-2T no. 40056 and J10 0-6-0 no. 65194, with their chimneys bagged, a routine precaution to keep out birds and rainwater. The J10 was of interest, being one of the last ex-Great Central locos to be seen here. No. 40056 was withdrawn week-ending 21st November and its companion two weeks later. (R. Humm coll.)

21. Inside 9E on 28th June 1967 two 8Fs nos 48332 and 48613 awaited their next turns of duty. The photographer was standing in the southerly bay and looking out onto part of the shed yard that was formerly roofed over. (T. Heavyside)

22. Trafford Park sorting sidings were seen on 3rd September 1968. MSC no. D4, Hudswell Clarke D1189 of 1960, was preparing to depart with a load of steel, from Sheffield perhaps, for a customer on the Estate. The view is to the northeast; in the background was the redundant loco shed and at right Old Trafford Stadium. Closer to, note the gaslight and the four-doll shunting signal. Mechanical signalling lasted in the yard until 1985. (B. Roberts)

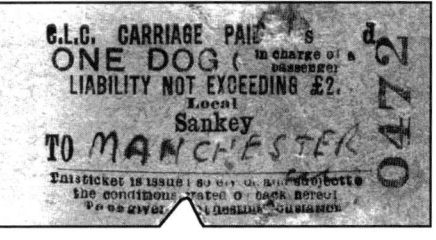

23. The last in a long line of steam shunters on the Estate was Andrew Barclay 0-4-0ST no. 1964 of 1929 at Brown & Polson, manufacturers of cornflour since 1854 and at the time of this picture, circa 1969, a household name for its custard powder. Here the loco was busying itself with some coal wagons and it continued in use until around 1977. In 2024 it could be found at the Lincolnshire Wolds Railway. (D. Phillips)

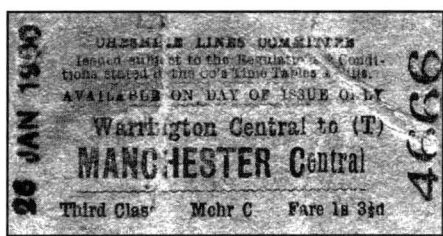

24. On 8th October 1986 no. 31454 approached Trafford Park West Junction with the 13.45 Liverpool – Sheffield. The two lower tracks coming in on the right served the remains of the goods yard where the Euroterminal was later built. In the background was an overhead wiring train awaiting its next assignment. Behind that was the transhipment shed, forerunner of the Manchester International Freight Terminal, whilst in the right background was the FLT. This opened in 1969 and had eight roads served by a gantry crane. (T. Heavyside)

25. After MSC ceased its railway activities in 1984 Trafford Park Estates hired in diesel shunters from British Rail and other parties. One such was no. 08669 which on 17th August 1992 hauled five wagons from the steel yard of Castle Services and four bogie tankers containing starch from Cerestar, successor to Brown & Polson, along Trafford Park Road. The tarpaulins on the four steel flats read Railfreight Metals Cardiff Rod Mill. (P. D. Shannon)

26. This was the view from the east end of the Euroterminal on 7th October 1993 soon after opening. The CLC line was behind the fence at left, inside which were two reception roads. The crane spanned five roads on four of which were posed a class 90 electric loco. The road nearest the camera continued beyond the terminal to Barton Dock. Euroterminal initially replaced the FLT but both terminals were required after 1998. On a typical day in 2024 there were 10 trains in and out of Trafford Park, serving the ports of Felixstowe, London Gateway and Southampton. (P.D. Shannon)

27. This was the Barton Dock Containerbase on 20th October 2011 shortly before its closure, after which the business transferred to the Euroterminal. No. 09002 had tailed the 04.20 ex-Felixstowe service from Trafford Park. The gleaming dome in the background belonged to the Trafford Centre, then the UK's third largest shopping mall, which opened in 1998. (P.D. Shannon)

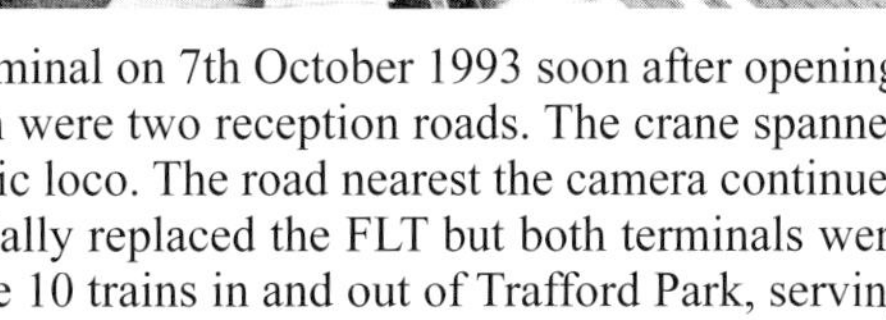

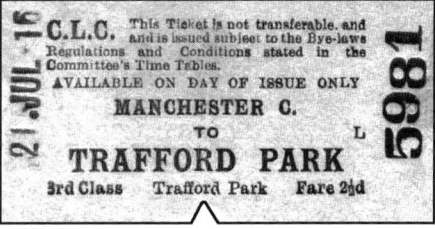

TRAFFORD PARK

Trafford Park station is 3¼ miles from Oxford Road and one mile beyond Trafford Park West Junction. It opened on 4th January 1904 in open countryside; the area subsequently became urbanised. The station was called Trafford Park & Stretford from c1926 until 6th May 1974. It occupies an elevated position where the railway crosses Moss Road. A ticket office was provided at street level with shelters on the platforms.

↗ 28. Class 5MT 4-6-0 no. 44725 ran in from Manchester Central with a down stopper on 17th April 1964 to pick up a good crowd, probably on their way home from work. The timber shelters looked comparatively recent, and the lightweight nature of the platforms was apparent. Trafford Park Station signal box was visible behind the locomotive. This, along with the boxes at Trafford Park Junction and Urmston closed on 2nd August 1971 when control passed to Manchester London Road PSB. In 2023 the station seemed windswept and neglected with minimal shelters offering meagre comfort. (A. Gilbert/R Humm coll.)

The street level ticket office was seen circa 2015 whilst in use by a taxi company. In spring 2023 it underwent refurbishment before reopening as a community wellbeing hub. (R. Greenhalgh)

HUMPHREY PARK

Humphrey Park opened on 15th October 1984 half a mile beyond Trafford Park to serve a district of post-WWII housing. It was funded by Greater Manchester Passenger Transport Executive. It had two platforms each with a basic shelter at its west end. Access was by ramped footpaths linked to the local roads Chatsworth Road and Derbyshire Lane West.

↓ 29. On 29th September 2009 TPE DMU no. 185113 ran through with the 12.47 Scarborough – Liverpool. Note the featureless platforms, not untypical of their era. (A.C.Hartless)

↑ *Shortly afterwards Northern DMU no. 150150 pulled away with the 14.27 Liverpool – Manchester Oxford Road revealing the up side shelter, identical to the one on the opposite platform. (A.C.Hartless)*

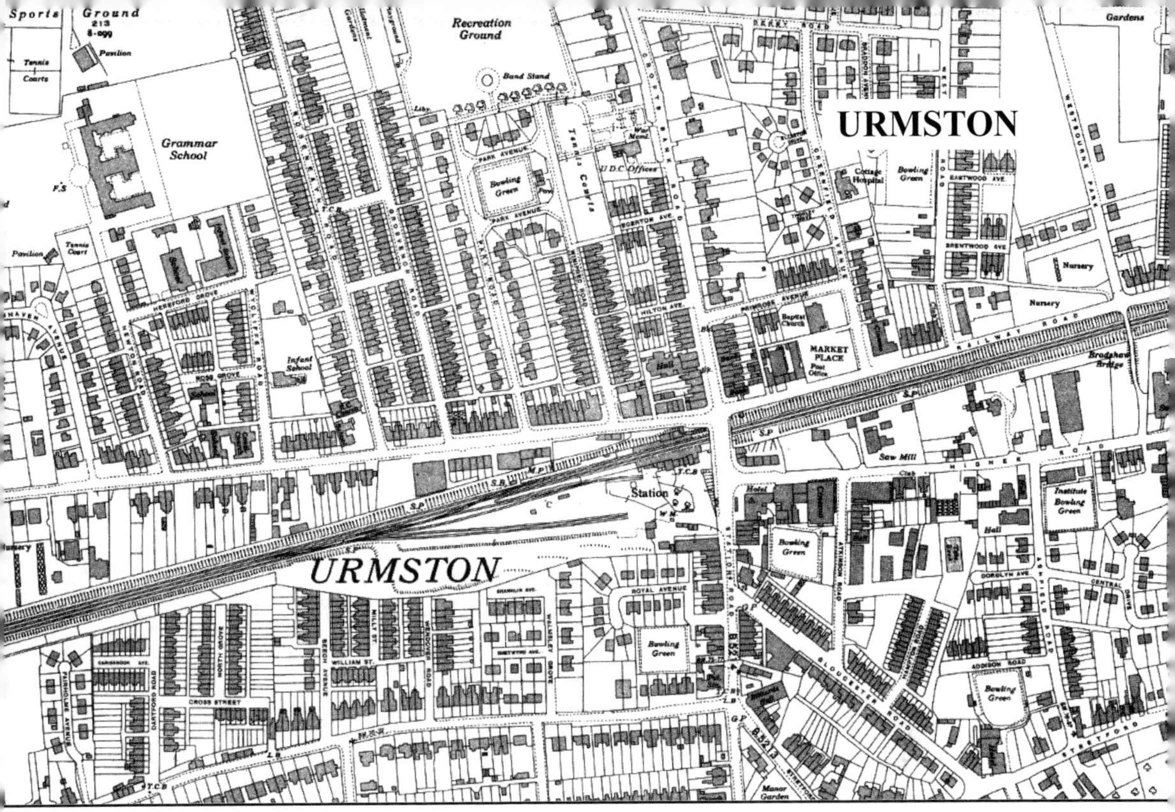

VI. Urmston has early medieval origins and was a small farming village until the railway arrived in 1873. It was originally the first station on the line after Manchester Central from which it was 4¾ miles distant. The railway led to rapid growth and the station was enlarged in 1889 when a new booking office was built on the bridge. At the 2011 census the population was 41,825.

30. This postcard image dated from around 1906 and showed a crowd of passengers awaiting the train to Manchester, which was arriving behind a tank engine running bunker first. The train was opposite the goods station. This had no shed, in common with most of the stations on our route, and closed from 29th October 1966. The train was obscuring the signal box. (P. Laming coll.)

31. The main building was on the south side of the tracks and its exterior was seen in the early 20th century. The two-storey section at left was the station master's accommodation. This twin-pavilion plan was used extensively on the MS&L and was the basis of most of the original stations on the CLC main line. The building fell out of use after a new entrance opened circa 1988 but was tenanted in mid-2008 and, in 2024, housed a popular bar and restaurant. (P. Laming coll.)

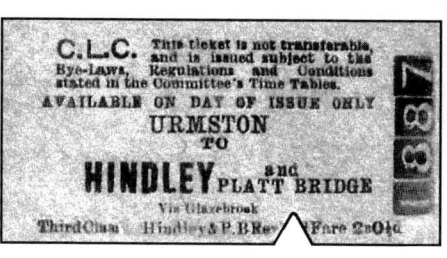

32. The new entrance was built on the north side of the station and was seen here on 28th March 2017 as Northern DMU no. 156459 arrived with the 08.55 Liverpool – Manchester Oxford Road. This view corresponds closely with picture no. 30. (P. Whatley)

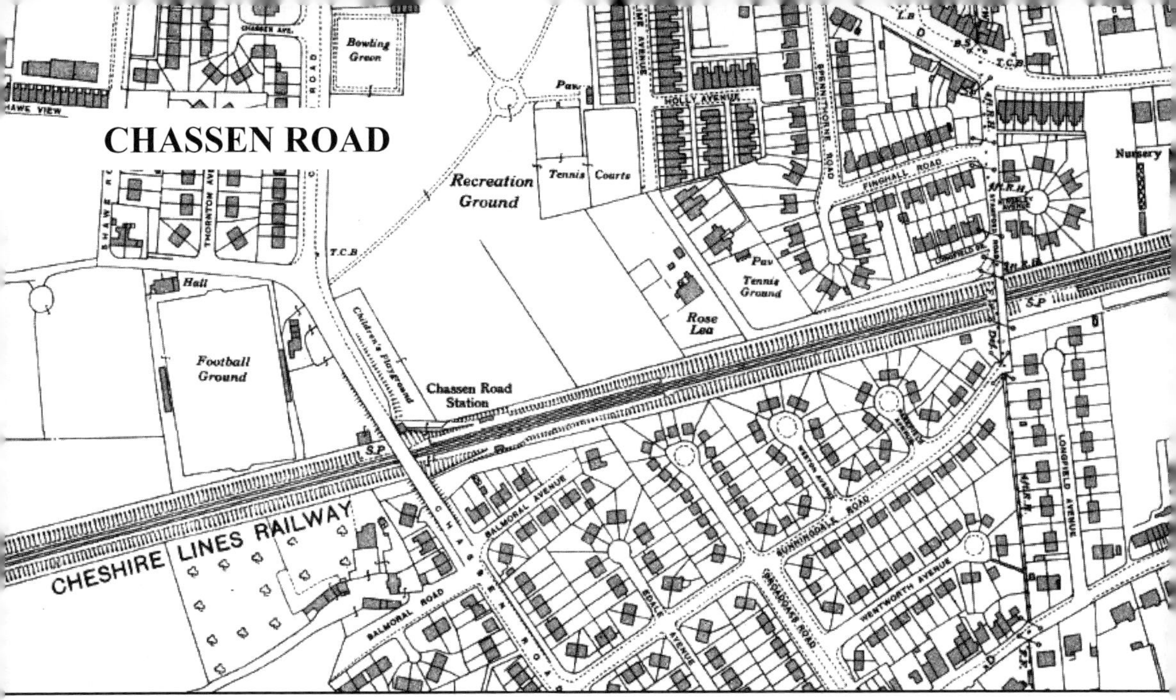

CHASSEN ROAD

VII. Chassen Road opened on 10th September 1934. It is half a mile from Urmston.

33. On 30th October 1992 Regional Railways Express DMU no. 158764 ran past with the 10.26 Middlesbrough – Liverpool. The up side shelter had been placed directly in front of its predecessor. The shelters underwent at least one further iteration during the following 30 years. (A.C. Hartless)

← On the same date the street level ticket office was recorded. The platforms were reached by ramps. (A.C. Hartless)

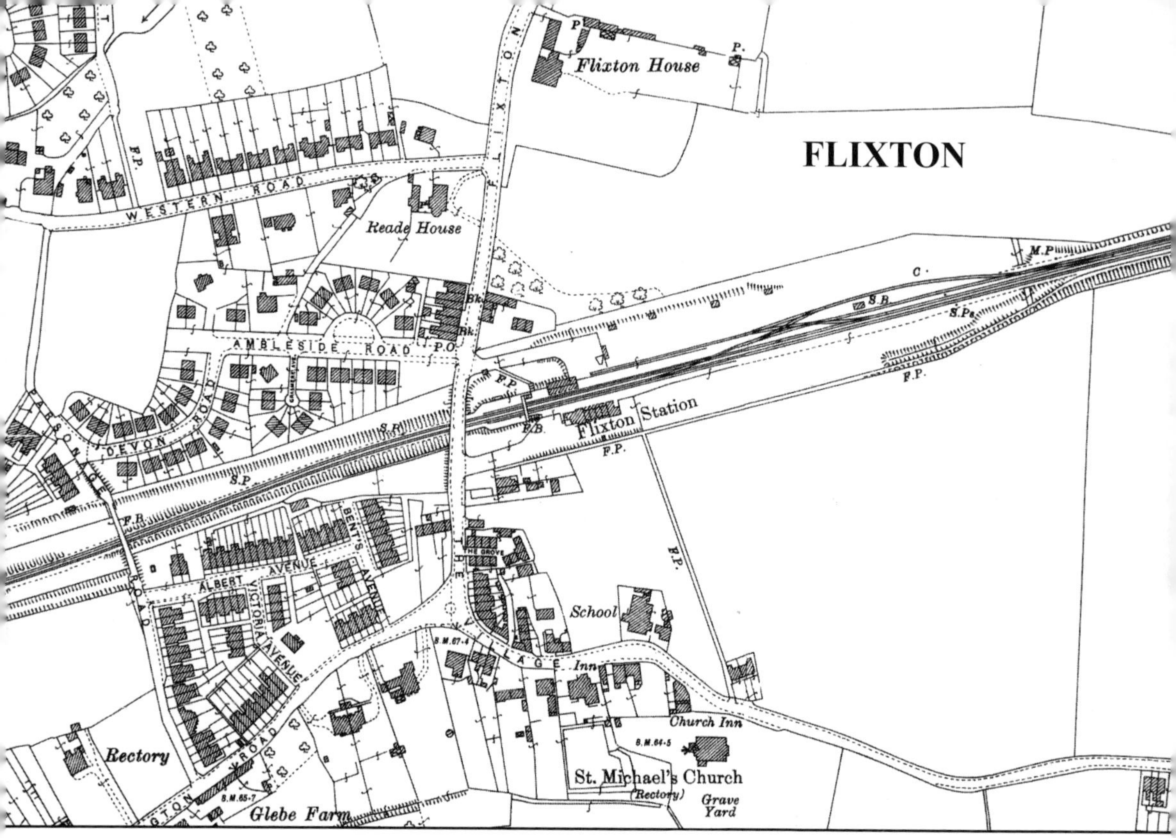

FLIXTON

VIII. The earliest record of Flixton is dated 1190. It remained a dispersed agricultural community until the arrival of the CLC when its population was around 1,500. The map of 1926 showed the spread of modern housing had only recently begun. By 2001 the population had risen gradually to 9,500. The station, 6 miles from Manchester Central, opened on 1st October 1873, four weeks after the opening of the line. Goods facilities were withdrawn from 2nd December 1963 and the signal box closed from 24th April 1966.

34. A westward view from around 1905 recorded the structures including the footbridge and gaslights. The trackwork in the foreground linked the running lines with the two goods sidings, one of which had its western end at the dock on the right-hand side. Note the track curving to the left beyond the bridge, marking the end of the three mile straight from Trafford Park and the start of the Ship Canal deviation. (P. Laming coll.)

35. Another westward view from circa 1912 captured GC class 11A 4-4-0 no. 871 calling with a Liverpool Central – Manchester Central semi-fast. Note the grounded coach body adjacent to the goods yard entrance on the right. (P. Laming coll.)

36. The station building became surplus to railway requirements and was sold to the hospitality sector in the early 1990s. In November 1998 it caught fire. The remains were demolished in 2001 leaving only the footbridge as a link with better times. On 29th September 2009 East Midlands DMU no. 158854 ran through with the 09.57 Norwich – Liverpool. (A.C. Hartless)

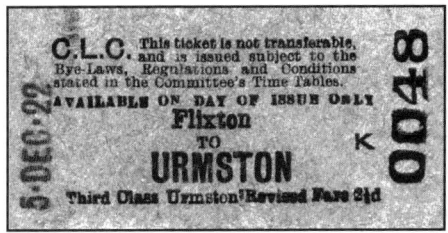

WEST OF FLIXTON

When the line was built it crossed the River Irwell immediately north of its confluence with the River Mersey. When the Manchester Ship Canal was constructed it canalised the Irwell and required a clearance level of 75 feet for over-bridges. Consequently the CLC had to build a 2½ mile deviation immediately south of the original route with a gradient of 1:135 on either side of the new Irlam Viaduct. This opened to goods from 9th January 1893 and to passengers from 26th March following. The viaduct is 1¼ miles west of Flixton during which the Manchester conurbation is left behind.

37. On 2nd November 1986 a class 108 DMU approached Irlam Viaduct with the 14.20 Manchester Piccadilly – Liverpool. The short spans either side of the main girder were constructed as brick arches. These failed owing to subsidence when the canal was first filled and were replaced by girders. The viaduct was built to accommodate four tracks but has only ever borne two. (T. Heavyside)

EAST OF IRLAM

The deviation on the west side of Irlam Viaduct was a little over one mile and included Irlam station. One track of the original route was retained by the MSC to serve the CWS soap works, which opened in 1895 on the canal bank north of the railway. This was a major factory covering 15 acres, supplying soap, candles and associated products for the hundreds of Co-ops up and down the country. The line had its own passenger service, the so-called Soap Works Express which linked the factory with Irlam station where workers could connect with main line trains via a flight of steps within the station building. The line also made a junction with the MSC railway that ran alongside the canal from Salford to Partington until 1977.

In 1910, heavy industry arrived in the form of the Partington Steel & Iron Co. later known as Irlam Steelworks. It was located on a triangular site south of the CLC main line bordered by the Ship Canal, on which it had its own wharfage, and the Glazebrook – Skelton Junction line. Its raw materials mostly arrived via the canal although it was connected to the railway at Cadishead. In 1957 a new connection was made with the main line, trailing in a little west of Irlam station. Its bridge across Liverpool Road still stood disused in 2024, the steelworks having closed in stages between 1974-79.

↗ *(top right)* 38. The CLC main line including the west end of Irlam Viaduct was visible running across the right background of this view of the MSC railway at Partington North Basin on 11th March 1954. There were two trains on the left track, the nearer with Austerity 0-6-0ST MSC no. 85 (Vulcan Foundry works no. 5294 of 1945) and immediately beyond was 0-6-0T MSC no. 62 *St Petersburg* (Hudswell Clarke works no. 1060 of 1914). The photographer did not identify the loco on the right-hand track but it looked like one of Irlam Steelworks' Yorkshire Engine 0-6-0STs, quite new at this time. At its height the MSC railway fleet comprised around 90 steam locos. (R. Humm coll.)

➜ 39. Inside Irlam Steelworks in around 1955 0-4-0ST no. 19 (Robert Stephenson Hawthorn works no. 7808 of 1954) was seen with two ladle wagons, used for moving molten metal within the works. Diesels replaced steam power here in the second half of the 1950s.
(L. Sommerfield/ R. Humm coll.)

➜ 40. The Soap Works Express was seen on its final shift on 6th September 1959 heading for Irlam station. The venerable carriage was an ex-Midland Railway six-wheeler and the 0-6-0ST was one of the Co-op's small fleet of Pecketts. Behind it an ex-LMS class 5MT 4-6-0 was climbing to Irlam Viaduct with an up express, and beyond that was Irlam Steelworks. (Hamilton Davies Trust)

IRLAM

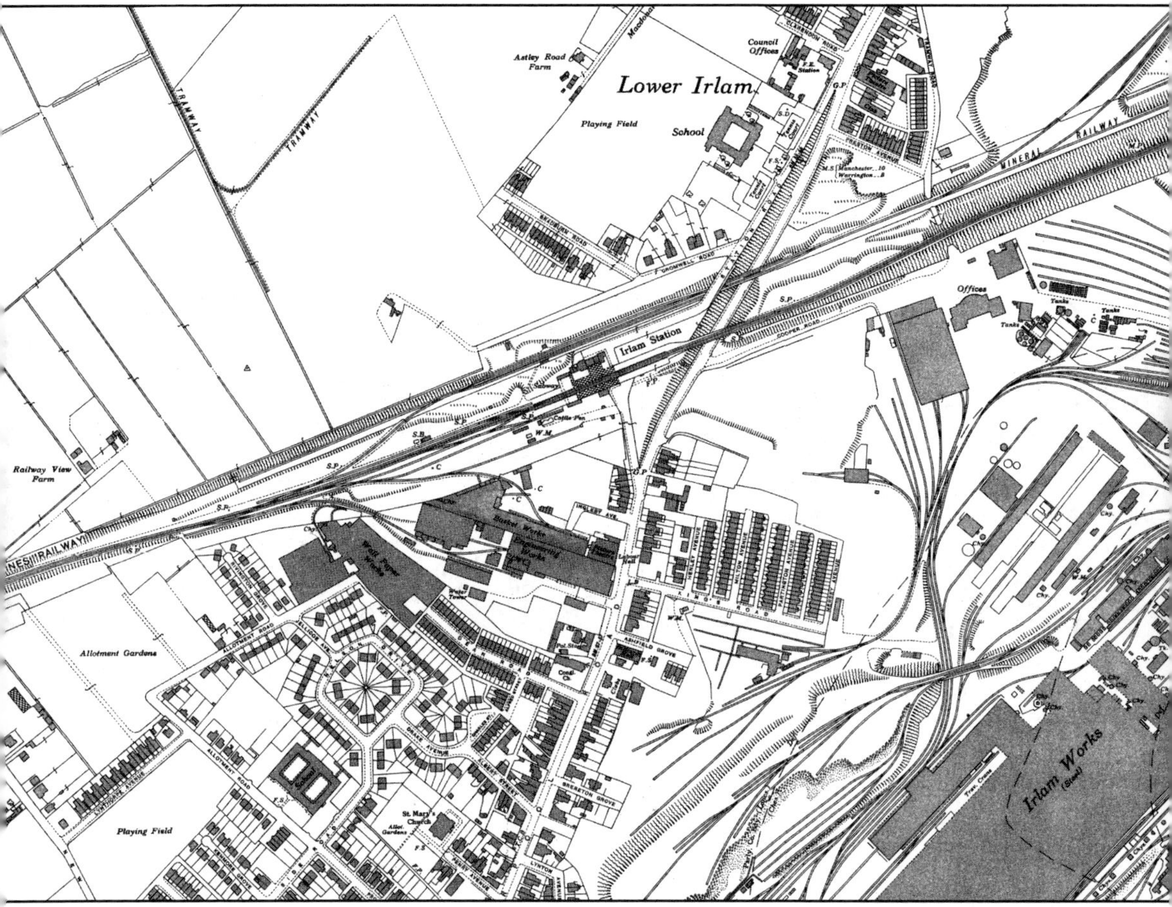

IX. Irlam can trace its antecedents to the 13th century but was never of consequence until the arrival of the railway. The station was 8 miles from Castlefield Junction and opened with, or soon after, the line. It was renamed Irlam & Cadishead from 1st August 1879 and Irlam for Cadishead during 1954 before reverting to Irlam from 6th May 1974. Irlam's population in 2011 was almost 20,000.

The main building, dating from the relocation of 1893, was retired from railway business around 1983 when it was boarded up and fenced off, shorn of its canopies, and a mean shelter provided instead. Happily, the Friends of Irlam Station, supported by the Hamilton Davies Trust, took on its restoration, and in March 2015 the building reopened as The Station, Café Bar & Heritage Hub with a strong railway theme. Subsequent attractions were added comprising the Station Art Park and the Signal Yard. It was announced in late 2023 that two passenger lifts were to be installed to access the subway beneath the tracks.

The mineral railway shown on the map was the route of the Soap Works Express.

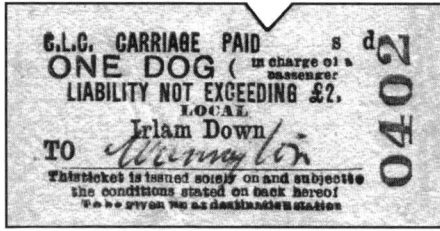

41. This eastward view was taken in 1892 during the construction of the replacement station. The original station was on the left with buildings similar to Flixton's and a goods dock on the down side. Beyond the station the line was bridged by the Manchester – Liverpool road, later the A57; the deviation carried the railway over the road. The new three-storey station building was taking shape on the right, backing onto the original alignment with the embankment for the deviation line, level with the middle floor, represented by the heap of earth at far right. (Hamilton Davies Trust)

42. This undated westward image illustrated the second station in the steam era. A train had just departed towards Glazebrook and a light engine was on the up line with the signal box beyond. The lower of the two semaphores on the down line controlled movements into the goods yard, which closed from 7th November 1966. The signal box closed on 2nd August 1971, and the westbound platform building was lost to a fire on 23rd July 1997. (R. Humm coll.)

43A. The Art Park included a short length of track on which were exhibited 0-4-0ST Peckett no. 2027 of 1942, formerly at UKAEA Windscale and which arrived here in 2020 from Carnforth, and three wagons representing local industry. The loco bore the name *Irlam* and carried the legend 'CWS Soap & Candle Works' on its cabside although it never worked there. The trucks comprised a 10T MSC dropside plank wagon, a tank wagon carrying livery CWS Ltd Margarine Works Higher Irlam, and a ladle wagon from Partington Steel & Iron Co. They were seen on 1st September 2023. The view was eastward with the main line parallel behind the hedge at right and the station behind the photographer. (A.C. Hartless)

43B. A westward view on the same date gave an indication of the bistro atmosphere on a sunny day and of the high quality of restoration of the station building. The Signal Yard in the background was focused round the ex-Midland Railway signal box from Keighley Station Junction which was relocated here in 2019. The up platform was behind the fence.
(A.C. Hartless)

EAST OF GLAZEBROOK

The descent from Irlam Viaduct ended before Glazebrook East Junction, which was ⅞ mile from Irlam. This was created when our route from Cornbrook Junction met the line from Skelton Junction to Cressington. The Skelton Junction line linked up with the MS&L's Woodhead route to Sheffield and beyond and, for much of its existence, carried a heavy freight traffic. Like our route it required a deviation to cross the Manchester Ship Canal, via Partington Viaduct, and as at Irlam the original low-level line was retained as far as the canal. After withdrawal of local passenger trains between Stockport Tiviot Dale and Liverpool Central from 30th November 1964 the new line was singled, and it closed entirely after the last goods train on 29th July 1982. The truncated old line lasted longer, originally serving Irlam Steelworks and latterly other industries at Partington North Basin, particularly petrochemicals, until 29th September 1999. The busy CLC signal box at Glazebrook East Junction was replaced in 1961 by a flat-roofed LMR box with 80 levers which in 2024 controlled the section of our route between the Manchester ROC and the Warrington Central signalling areas.

44. On 21st June 1957 3MT 2-6-2T no. 40097 coasted into Glazebrook with the 2.48pm Manchester Central – Warrington Central. East Junction was in the background where the Skelton Junction new line could be seen curving to the right. An O4 2-8-0 looked to be awaiting the road from the Exchange Sidings, which were located between the new and old lines of the Skelton Junction route. Behind that were some of the structures of Irlam Steelworks. The signal box was barely visible behind the bracket signal on the up line. (B. Brooksbank)

45. Twenty-nine years later, on 4th April 1986, in a view from the opposite direction, no. 37023 propelled its train of nine empty petroleum tankers onto the up line for their return working to Haverton Hill, Teesside. They had been discharged at a terminal on the site of the original Cadishead station. This was the last regular traffic onto the Skelton Junction line. In 2024 all that remained of Glazebrook East Junction was the two main running lines, the down loop, a trailing crossover, the signal box – and a lot more trees. (P.D. Shannon)

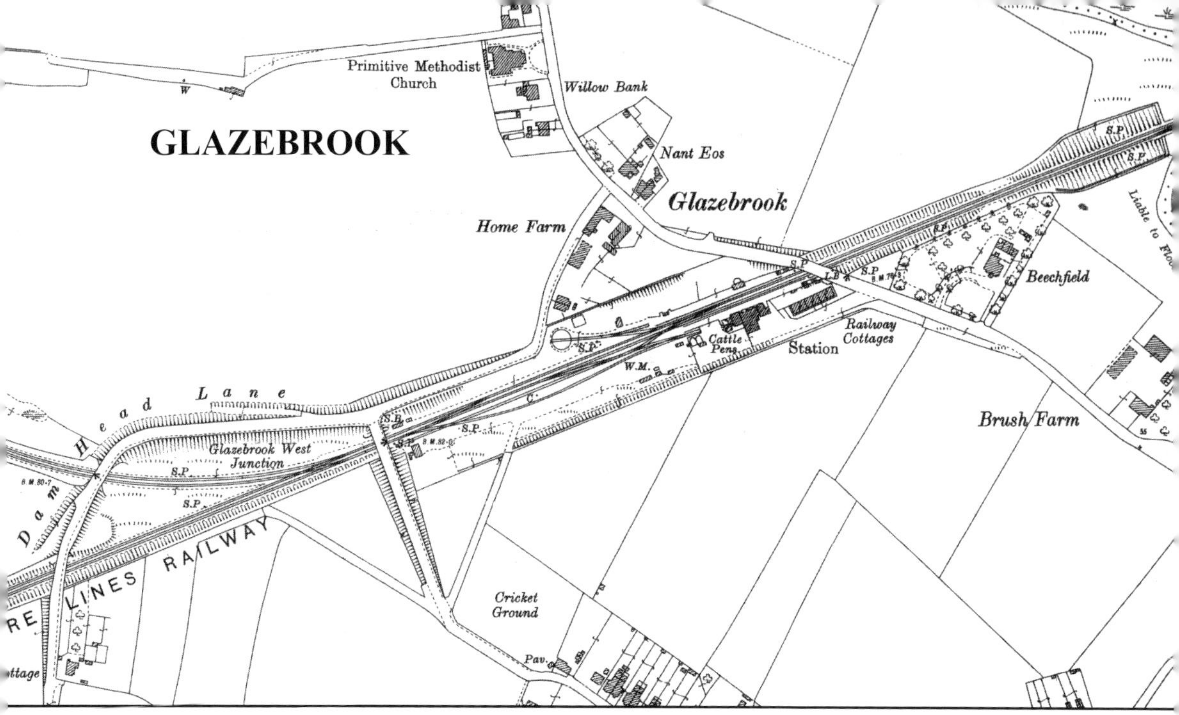

GLAZEBROOK

X. Glazebrook was a dispersed village in the parish of Warrington when the railway arrived, and in 2024 the population of Rixton-with-Glazebrook was still only around 2,000. The Glaze Brook, which our route crosses between Glazebrook East Junction and the station, forms the boundary between Greater Manchester and Warrington; it flows south into the Mersey. Glazebrook was 9¾ miles from Manchester Central.

46. On 21st June 1957 class O4/8 2-8-0 no. 63721 of Gorton shed steamed past with a westbound train comprising 15 loaded tipplers. This may well have been the same train seen in the background of picture no. 44. We could see the full extent of the goods facilities, which were withdrawn from 3rd August 1964; on this date the occupants were cattle trucks. Note at extreme right the short access road to the down side facilities from Glazebrook Lane, the B5212, also an up passenger train departing under the bridge. The map showed a turntable on the up side which had evidently been removed by the time of this picture. (B. Brooksbank)

47. Looking west on 20th June 1964, 4MT 2-6-4T no. 42456, a long-term resident of Wigan Springs Branch, was seen working a Wigan Central – Manchester Central stopper. This service ceased from 2nd November 1964. In the background was Glazebrook West Junction signal box, a CLC installation on a tall stone base giving the signaller a clear view over the road bridge. This marked the start of the MS&L branch line to Wigan Central, which opened initially on 16th October 1879 for goods to Strangeways & Hindley and was extended to Wigan on 1st April 1884 when the passenger service began. It closed from 22nd April 1968 when the box was abolished. (Rail-online.co.uk)

48. At the time of writing Glazebrook was one of the least altered stations on the CLC main line 150 years after its construction. On 6th July 2023 Northern DMUs nos 156425 and 150139 were recorded passing with the 17.46 Manchester Oxford Road – Liverpool. This service called at all stops between Manchester and Warrington, except Glazebrook. Note the ornamental drinking fountain set into the brickwork near the righthand margin. All the original stations on the route had one, evidently a job lot, all stamped with the date 1872 the year before the line opened. (D. Birmingham)

West of Glazebrook

The GC opened a west to north curve on 1st July 1900 which left the CLC at Dam Lane Junction. This allowed through running from the Liverpool direction onto the Wigan Central branch. The curve closed from 11th May 1965 but the signal box lasted until 25th November 1973.

ROF RISLEY

When the CLC main line opened, the 4¼ miles between Glazebrook and Padgate were uninhabited peat bog. This was still largely the case 66 years later when WWII broke out and 927 acres north of our route were chosen for the site of the Risley Royal Ordnance Factory, where bomb casings etc were filled with explosives. Most of the materiel was rail borne. The majority of the workforce was also transported by train to a non-timetable station of three platforms, one on the CLC up line, with the other two served by a loop line on the up side. There was also a separate branch with its own terminus from Newchurch on the Wigan Central line. After hostilities ceased, parts of the site were used in the development of the UK's nuclear weapons and power generation programmes, but these activities were gradually relocated elsewhere. The rail connection with the CLC closed from 6th April 1964.

49. This was an undated eastward view of the principal station at ROF Risley. The factory site was out of view to the left and was accessed by the substantial footbridge crossing the reception sidings in the centre background. The two loop lines were separated by the broad island platform, which was provided with a large umbrella canopy. A rake of passenger stock occupied the right-hand road. The structure just visible above the canopy was the southward continuation of the footbridge, evidently a later addition, to the third platform. The latter served the CLC up line, the position of which can be gauged from the three lamp posts on the right. (British Railways)

BIRCHWOOD

Birchwood began its life in 1968 when Warrington Development Corporation purchased a large site bordered by the CLC to the south, the M6 motorway to the west and the M62 (opened in 1974) to the north, much of it previously belonging to ROF Risley. Birchwood was created as a new town within the Borough of Warrington. By 2001 it had a population of around 12,000. Its station opened officially on 6th October 1980 just under 3 miles from Glazebrook.

50. On 24th May 1986 no. 31426 called with the 13.45 Liverpool – Sheffield. The original covered footbridge, which doubled as a right of way, dominated the view. The bridge in the background carried the M6 which opened in 1965. (T. Heavyside)

51. On 4th May 2023 East Midlands Railway DMUs nos 170517 and 170509 formed the 09.55 Norwich – Liverpool, seen passing Birchwood five hours into their journey. The second footbridge and associated lifts were installed in 2014. (P.D. Shannon)

PADGATE

XI. Padgate was a rural area of little significance until it became a parish in 1838. The coming of the railway gave it greater prominence and it developed into an eastern suburb of Warrington. It was a little under 14 miles from Manchester Central.

The 1926 map showed a one-road engine shed east of the station, which opened around the same time as the Warrington avoiding line and closed circa 1929. The avoider, also known as the Straight Line, diverged from the Warrington Central route at Padgate Junction ¼ mile west of the station. It ran directly to Sankey Junction between 13th August 1883 and 22nd July 1968, the official closure date.

Padgate was home to one of the RAF's main training centres between 1939-56. Located north of Padgate Junction, it is now mostly redeveloped.

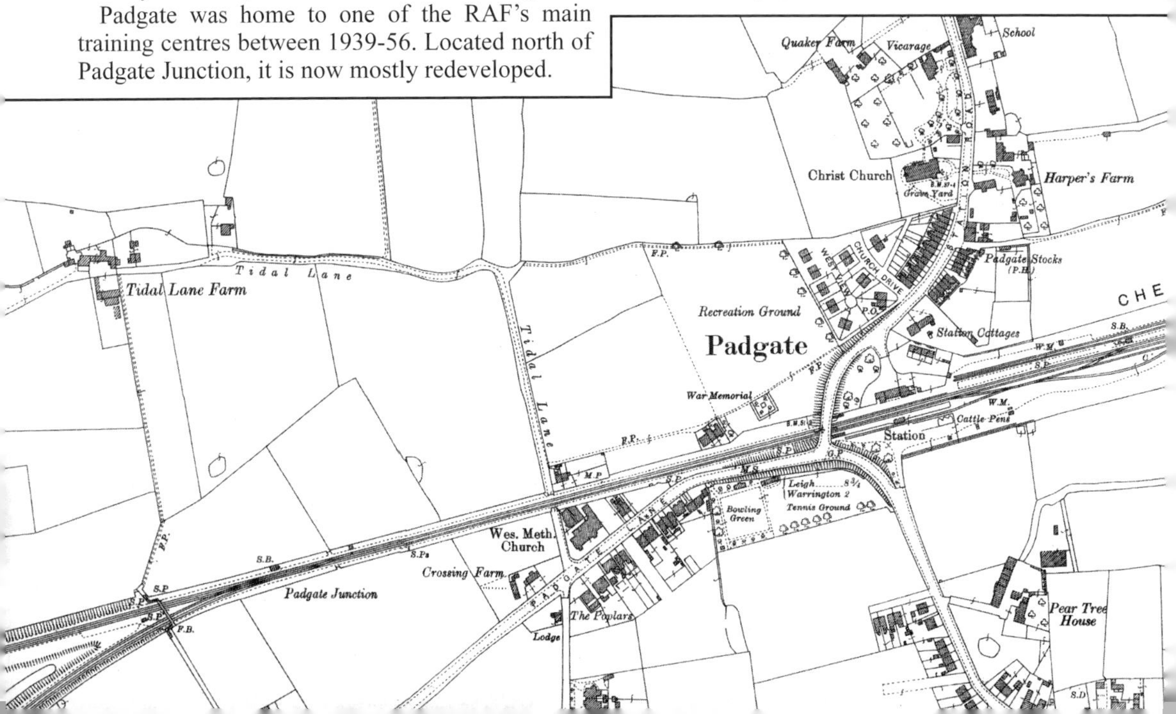

52. This Edwardian era postcard looked east as an up goods receded past the signal box. The siding provision was greater here than at the other stations we have visited so far. Note the cattle pen and the goods office. Goods facilities ceased from 9th August 1965. (R. Humm coll.)

53. This aerial view from 1934 also looked east. The obvious change from the earlier view was the concrete pipe factory that was in production until the 1960s. The station was still otherwise mostly surrounded by farmland, all of which was built over after WWII. (Britain from Above)

54. On 17th October 1953 5MT 4-6-0 no. 45455 was recorded departing with the 10.10 (SO) Warrington Central – Stockport Tiviot Dale. Former LMS types gradually replaced ex-Great Central motive power on the CLC after Nationalisation, although this example was a visitor from the ex-Caledonian Railway shed at Carlisle Kingmoor. The signal box was the second at the site and was commissioned on 11th March 1906. It had a 30-lever frame and was abolished on 26th February 1967. (E.D. Bruton/R. Humm coll.)

55. On 19th August 2019 Pacer DMU no. 142045 arrived with the 11.19 Liverpool – Manchester Oxford Road. The original station structures were still in situ, however the two recently installed shelters on the down platform signalled the end for the CLC building in between, which was demolished soon afterwards. Despite being unstaffed the up side station building looked well cared for. The former station house, the gable nearer the camera, became a fish and chip emporium in 2007. In 2021 it installed former Southern Railway bogie van no. S4588S on a short section of track behind the up platform opposite where the photographer was standing. This augmented the restaurant's seating capacity but was originally built to transport circus elephants.

The bus-bodied Pacers were introduced in 1985-86 and were becoming life expired by this time; withdrawals commenced soon afterwards. This unit found an imaginative new purpose in 2023 at Kirk Merrington Primary School in County Durham, one carriage housing the library and the other a wellbeing hub. (A.C. Hartless)

EAST OF WARRINGTON CENTRAL

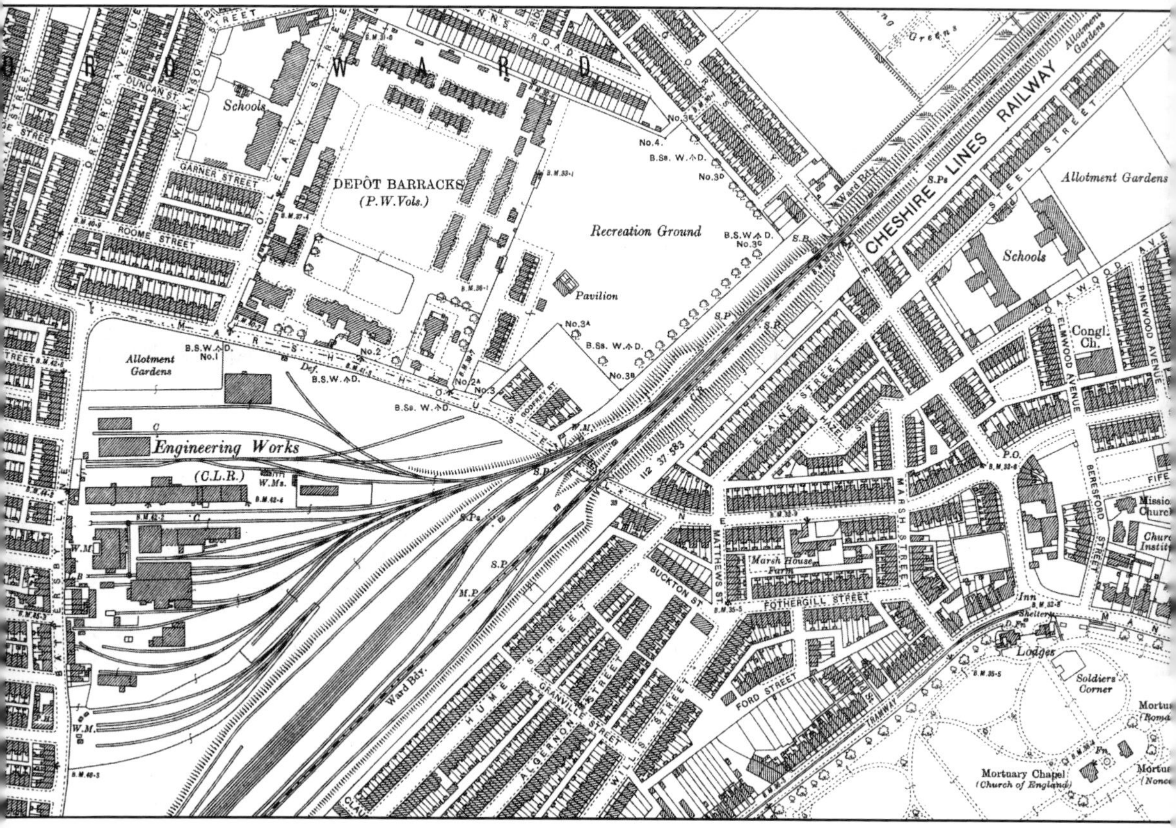

XII. Between Padgate Junction and Warrington Central the CLC built engineering workshops for purposes including track maintenance, signalling, printing and general stores. These were on the north side of the line and were in use from 1881 to 1936. Part of the site was then used by Carrington Iron Works until the mid-1960s. Movements in and out of the sidings were controlled by Workshops signal box on the up side of the main line from 1881-1973.

Warrington Central goods depot was immediately east of the station, also on the up side. It was replaced in 1897 by a three-storey warehouse and enlarged sidings. Movements in and out of the sidings were controlled by Warrington Sidings signal box on the up side of the main line from 1914-73. Public goods facilities closed from 1st October 1965 but company traffic, for example, Rylands Steel, continued into 1982. The warehouse received listed status and was redeveloped into the Grand Central Apartments. Some of the sidings were still used in 2024 for stabling DMUs and engineers' plant.

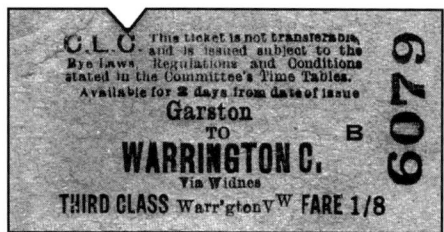 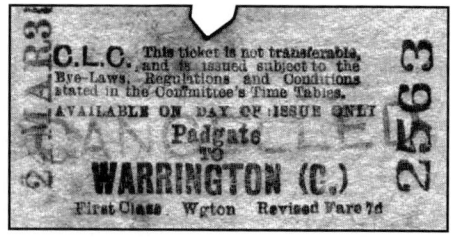

56. This was the southern part of the CLC's Warrington Works around 1910. The amount of timber suggested sleepers were an important product. All the CLC's signalling installations were made here from the late 1870s until 1930 when the work was transferred to the LMS. (P. Hanson coll.)

> **Views of Warrington Bank Quay can be found in**
> *Chester to Warrington*, *Crewe to Wigan* **and** *Liverpool to Runcorn*.

57. An open day was held at the goods depot on 10th October 1981 when nos 40115, 25085 and 08289, highly representative of contemporary motive power, were on display. The warehouse displayed with tasteful prominence 'Cheshire Lines' and each of its three founding partners. (T. Heavyside)

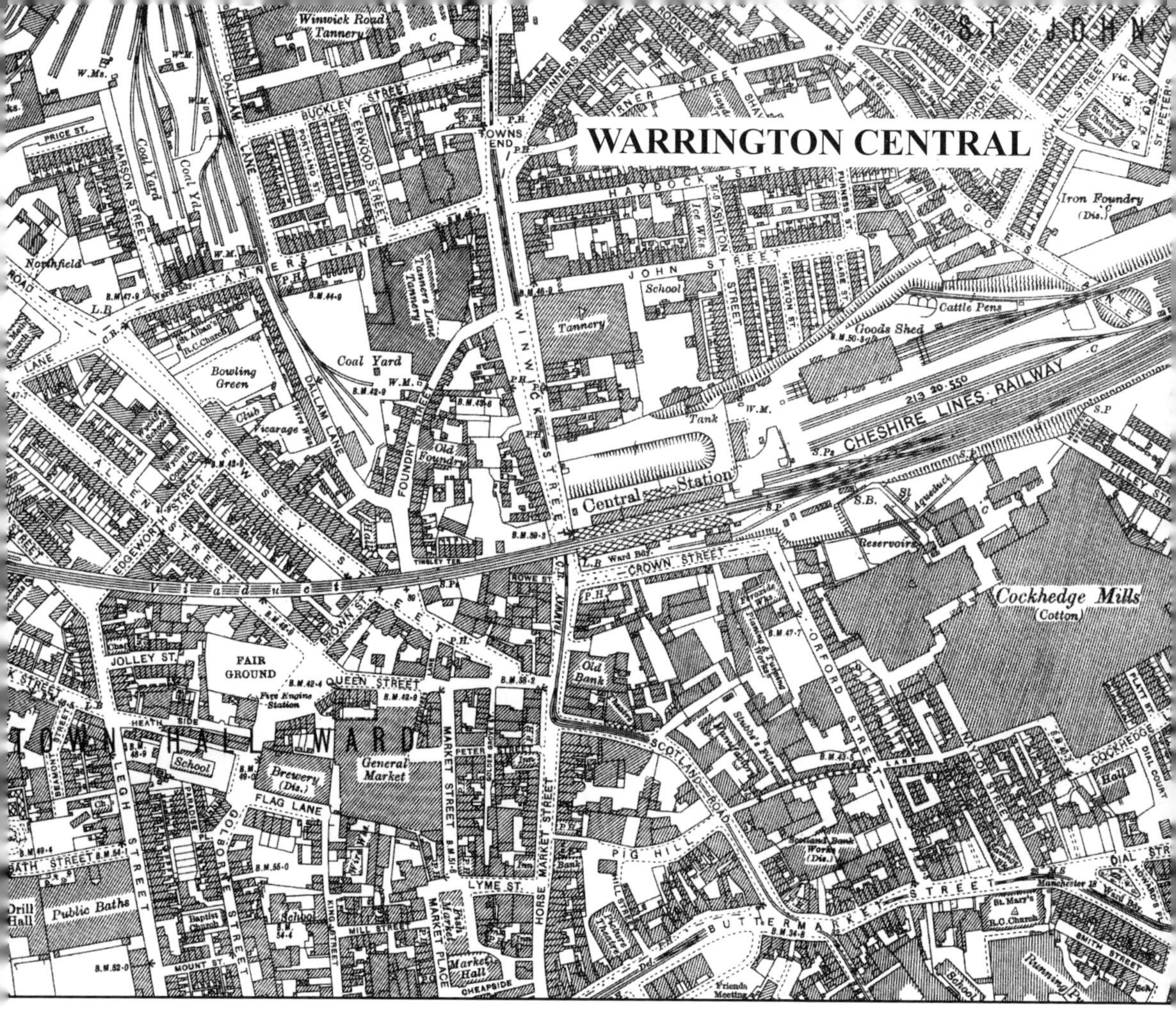

↓ 58. This eastward view was taken in 1929 and featured a brand-new Sentinel steam railcar on a demonstration run for a party of senior staff. The CLC operated four of these units until soon after the outbreak of WWII. They were the only exception to its policy of hiring its motive power from the LNER. At left could be seen the goods warehouse, and at right Warrington Station signal box. This was a 46-lever installation built at the nearby workshops in 1894 when it replaced an earlier example. The rightmost signal controlled movements from the locomotive siding. (T. Boothy coll./P.Hanson)

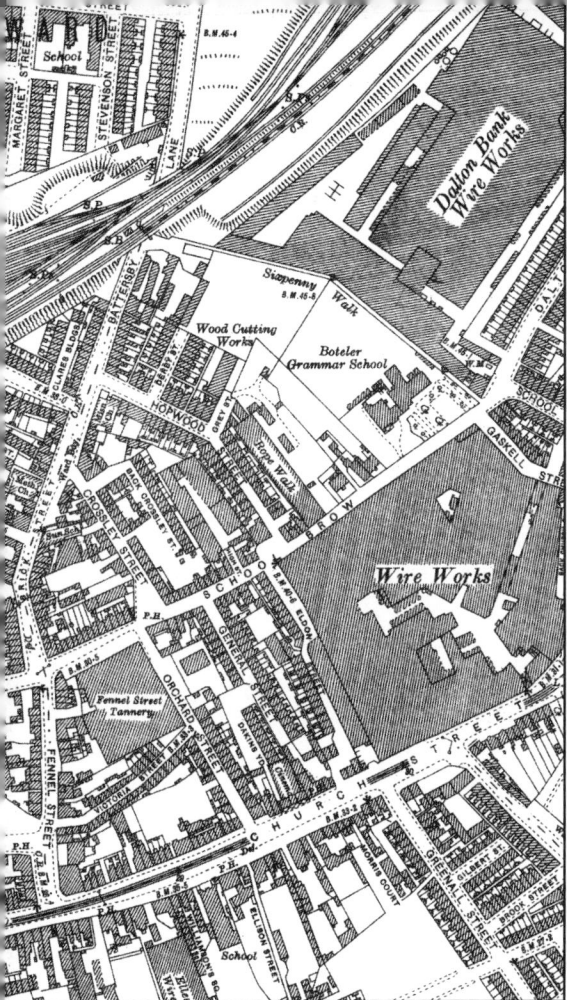

XIII. The CLC's initial plan was to build its main line directly from Padgate to Sankey with its Warrington station to be located at Dallam, but the town council requested the line be diverted in a southerly loop to bring the station ½ mile closer to the town centre. It was situated adjacent to Winwick Street, later the A49, just north of Horse Market Street, thereby justifying the suffix. It was 15¾ miles from Manchester Central and 18 miles and 30 chains from Liverpool Central.

The passenger station's main entrance was on the up side, facing away from the town centre; entrances were provided later to both platforms from Winwick Street. The main entrance was relocated in 1983 to a new building on Winwick Street. Passenger usage in 2017-18 was 1.764 million.

A basic one road engine shed was provided outside the south wall of the station. It was demolished in around 1938 and was not replaced, however up to three engines continued to be stabled there until the mid-60s when the facilities comprised a rudimentary coaling stage and an inspection pit.

↓ 59. On a day in c1973 the breakdown train appeared behind Brush Type 4 no. 1574 and was snapped from the signal box. The original ridge and furrow platform canopies had by then been replaced with the straight variety seen here. (D. Lennon)

60. On 13th October 1986 no. 31155 was recorded arriving with a Sheffield – Liverpool service. It was passing Warrington Central signal box, which was commissioned on 11th November 1973. This LMR standard 1950s box was previously located at Platt Bridge Junction near Wigan where it became redundant in 1971. It had a 55-lever frame and was still in use in 2024 when its fringe boxes were Glazebrook East Junction and Hunts Cross. (J. Whitehouse)

61A. This southward view from 1990 showed the BR Staff Association premises at left fronting Winwick Street, with the 1983 station entrance further along. This partially obscured the original CLC building which was elevated to be level with the tracks. The former main entrance was beneath the pediment at far left; this marked the halfway point of the building's length. The passenger facilities were almost all located on this side of the station which was linked to the Liverpool platform by a subway. Facilities originally included a refreshment room, in common with Manchester Central and Liverpool Central. The old building was leased to commercial tenants after 1983. (R. Humm coll.)

61B. Lifts were installed within the original buildings in 2008. In 2011 the station was redeveloped with a new entrance and a refurbished interior, as seen here on Easter Sunday, 31st March 2024. (D. Birmingham)

WEST OF WARRINGTON CENTRAL

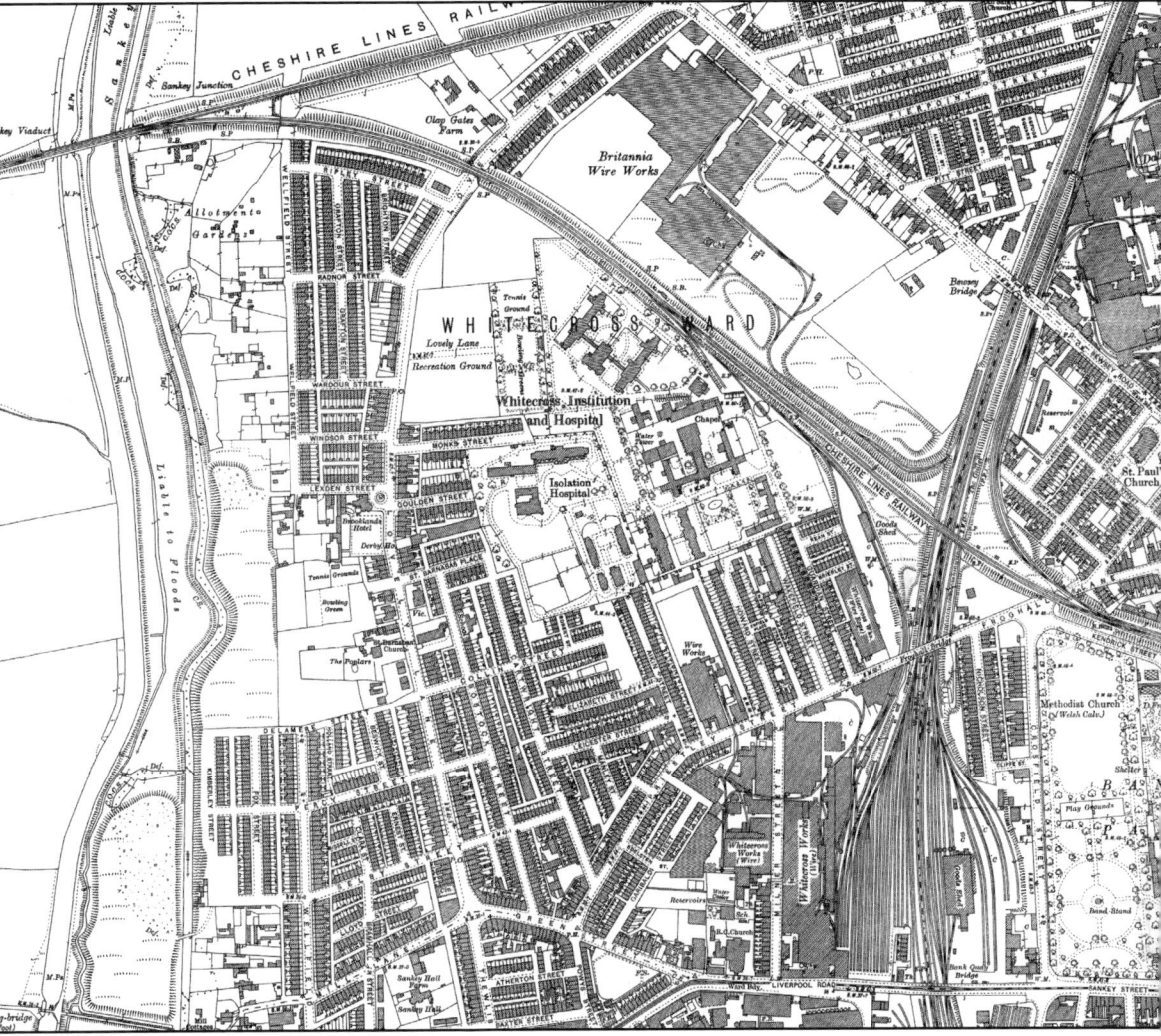

XIV. Now our route turns north westward to re-join the Straight Line at Sankey Junction. Leaving the station the line crosses the low-lying Warrington Viaduct. Beyond this the short Bewsey and Dallam Forges goods branch (1873-c1969) diverged northward shortly before the bridge across the former LNW main line to Wigan and the north. Following this, the Whitecross goods branch (c1874-c1970) trailed into the down line. Apart from serving the Whitecross Steel Works there was also a goods shed and a turntable, the nearest one to the station stabling point. Bewsey signal box (1930-73) stood on the up side close to Whitecross Junction and replaced two earlier boxes controlling the two goods branches.

There were three signal boxes at Sankey Junction. The first opened on the up side with the Straight Line on 13th August 1883. It was replaced in 1894 by a larger box on the opposite side of the tracks. This was itself replaced in 1943 by an Air Raid Precautions type box further west but also on the down side which lasted until 3rd March 1969 following the closure of the Straight Line. This was last used on 23rd June 1968 by an excursion that covered four different routes between Liverpool and Manchester behind two different steam locos including 8F 2-8-0 no. 48033 on the CLC leg.

Immediately beyond Sankey Junction our route crosses the Sankey Brook and the St Helens Canal, before the connection to USAF Burtonwood trailed into the up line between 1940-93. This carried heavy traffic during the war years; Burtonwood was the largest allied airfield in Europe in WWII with around 18,000 service personnel.

62. On 16th May 1989 no. 47434 *Pride in Huddersfield* passed the junction for the Burtonwood Airbase branch with the 16.20 Newcastle – Liverpool. The rear of the train was at the site of Sankey Junction whilst the fifth and sixth coaches were crossing Sankey Viaduct. The locomotive was coming level with the ground frame, which controlled movements on and off the branch. (A. Hart)

WARRINGTON WEST

Historically Warrington ended at Sankey Brook, but in the 21st century it began to spread westward, covering much of Burtonwood Airfield. Warrington West opened on 15th December 2019 to serve the districts of Great Sankey and Westbrook, and the cost quoted was £20.5m. It is 16¼ miles from Liverpool.

63. On 3rd July 2019, five months before the station opened, a pair of East Midlands class 158s, of which 158857 was the rear set, was seen running from Liverpool to Norwich. Note the main station building at extreme left and the height difference between it and the platforms. (P.D. Shannon)

64. On 12th March 2020 DMU no. 195102 arrived with the 11.22 Liverpool – Manchester Oxford Road. Class 195 represented the third generation of diesel trains on this route. They were built in Spain by CAF (Construcciones y Auxiliar de Ferrocarriles) and put to service on Northern routes in 2019-20 to replace the class 142 Pacers. (D. Birmingham).

SANKEY for PENKETH

XV. The station is close to the parish church of Great Sankey. Twenty years after the line's opening it was still a quiet dispersed village on the Warrington – Prescot road, later the A57. The area became fully urbanised in the late 20th century by which time it was contiguous with Warrington. The station lost almost its entire service following the opening of Warrington West, which is only ½ mile away, east of the Sycamore Lane bridge.

The station was initially called Sankey. The suffix 'for Penketh', one mile away to the southwest, was officially added by 1903 and, in 2024, the station was still referred to as such in timetables etc. However the signage on the station building was simply Sankey.

65. An early 20th century postcard looked eastward through the station, which was not dissimilar to others on our route. These structures still stood in 2024, along with a modern shelter on the up platform. Note the end of the goods siding at right; goods facilities were withdrawn from 5th November 1962. (P Laming coll.)

66. On 2nd August 1973 Brush Type 4 no. 1955 (soon to become TOPS no. 47511) ran through with empty cartics from Warrington Central, where there was a vehicle unloading ramp, to Knowle & Dorridge from where Jaguars and Land Rovers were despatched. Your compiler speculates the route taken was Brunswick (reverse), Cressington Junction and Speke Junction, thence Birmingham.

TOPS is the acronym for Total Operations Processing System, a computer system for managing railway rolling stock. It was developed in the 1960s in the USA and British Rail implemented it in 1973. It replaced manual records and, amongst other things, led to the complete renumbering of all BR's locomotives. (D. Lennon)

The previous picture was taken from the signal box steps around the same time as this view of the box itself. This all-brick cabin dated from mid-1918 when it replaced an earlier one. It was abolished on 16th December 1973. (D. Lennon)

EAST OF WIDNES

The 3¼ miles between Sankey and the next station are the furthest distance between stops on our route and are almost entirely straight. After 1¾ miles Widnes East Junction was created in April 1877 when the two-mile freight branch to Widnes was opened. There were three signal boxes here, the first from 1878-91, the second 7½ chains further west from 1891-1956, and the third, an LMR type, 1956-87. At the site of the junction our route in 2024 passed the boundary between the boroughs of Warrington and Halton.

Half a mile beyond Widnes East Junction was the short-lived Widnes West Junction where a west to south curve accessed the Widnes branch from the Liverpool direction. This was no longer needed after the Widnes Central loop was completed from Hough Green in 1879. After a further ½ mile, our route passed beneath the St Helens & Runcorn Gap Railway (SH&RG, 1833-1981) ¼ mile south of its Farnworth & Bold station, which closed in 1951 (for more details, see *Liverpool to Runcorn*); this line was superseded by the A557 Watkinson Way in 1994. West of this bridge was the 140yd Farnworth Tunnel that was opened out circa 1893.

WIDNES
(formerly FARNWORTH and WIDNES NORTH)

XVI. Farnworth was first recognised by a charter of 1352 and was an agricultural village until the railway age. Its population in 2004 was 6,300. The CLC station was known at different times as Farnworth for Widnes, Farnworth for Appleton, and Farnworth (Widnes), partly to avoid confusion with a) Farnworth & Bold on the SH&RG, and b) Farnworth on the L&Y Manchester & Bolton line. British Railways renamed it Widnes North from 5th January 1959 (and at the same time renamed the former SH&RG's station in the centre of Widnes, 1¼ miles away, to Widnes South). From 6th May 1968 the CLC station became simply Widnes, Widnes South having closed in 1962. Paul Simon's song 'Homeward Bound', a top seller in 1966, is said to have been written here whilst he awaited a train to Hull. Goods facilities, which included a warehouse and a 5-ton crane, were located on the up side west of the passenger station until their withdrawal from 6th July 1964.

C.L.C. CARRIAGE PAID
ONE DOG (in charge of a passenger)
LIABILITY NOT EXCEEDING £2.
FOREIGN
Farnworth Un
TO Northallerton
This ticket is issued solely on and subject to the conditions stated on back hereof
To be given up at destination station
0087

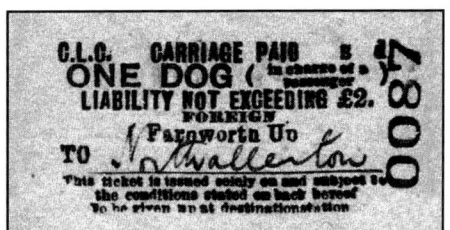

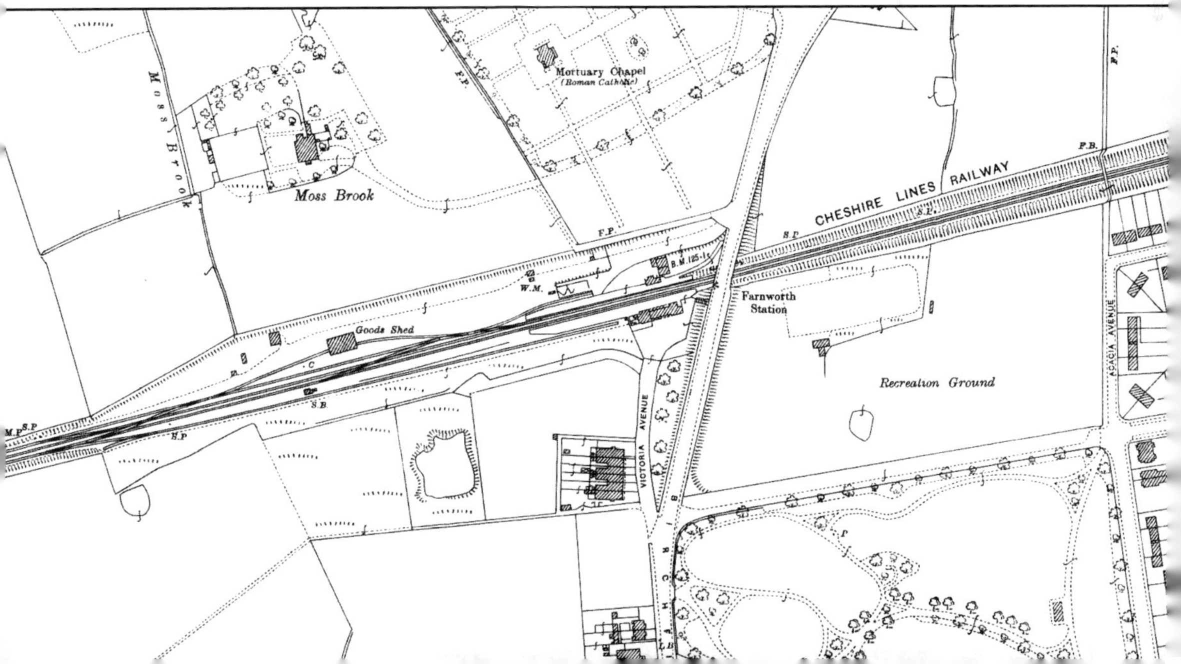

67. This is an eastward view of circa 1910 and revealed Farnworth to be another standard CLC station of 1872-73 right down to the drinking fountain. The train appeared to be a Manchester – Liverpool express hauled by GC class 13 4-2-2 no. 972. A footbridge was subsequently added to link the platforms. (B. Kelsall/P. Laming coll.)

68. This westward view from the footbridge captured 2MT 2-6-0 no. 46516 passing with a private charter for former employees of the CLC on 2nd July 1966 to celebrate the railway's centenary. In the left background could be seen Widnes North signal box which replaced the first installation here in 1904 and was abolished from 8th October 1967. The goods station was located behind the train but all that remained was a loading gauge. (G. Howarth)

69. On 8th July 2019, DMU no. 195116 ran through with the 11.16 Liverpool – Manchester Airport. Note the modern safety fencing at left separating the building from the platform. (D. Birmingham)

HOUGH GREEN

XVII. Hough Green was first shown in the timetable for May 1874 and is 1¾ miles of straight track from Widnes (Farnworth). Hough Green was merely a hamlet until the 1950s when residential development began in earnest ultimately linking the districts of Ditton, Hough Green and Upton. The station was known as Hough Green for Ditton between 1894 and 1974. The LNW station at Ditton Junction was just 1 mile further south. The Widnes Central loop trailed in ¼ mile east of the station. Travelling westward, Hough Green was the last of the by now familiar CLC main line twin pavilion stations.

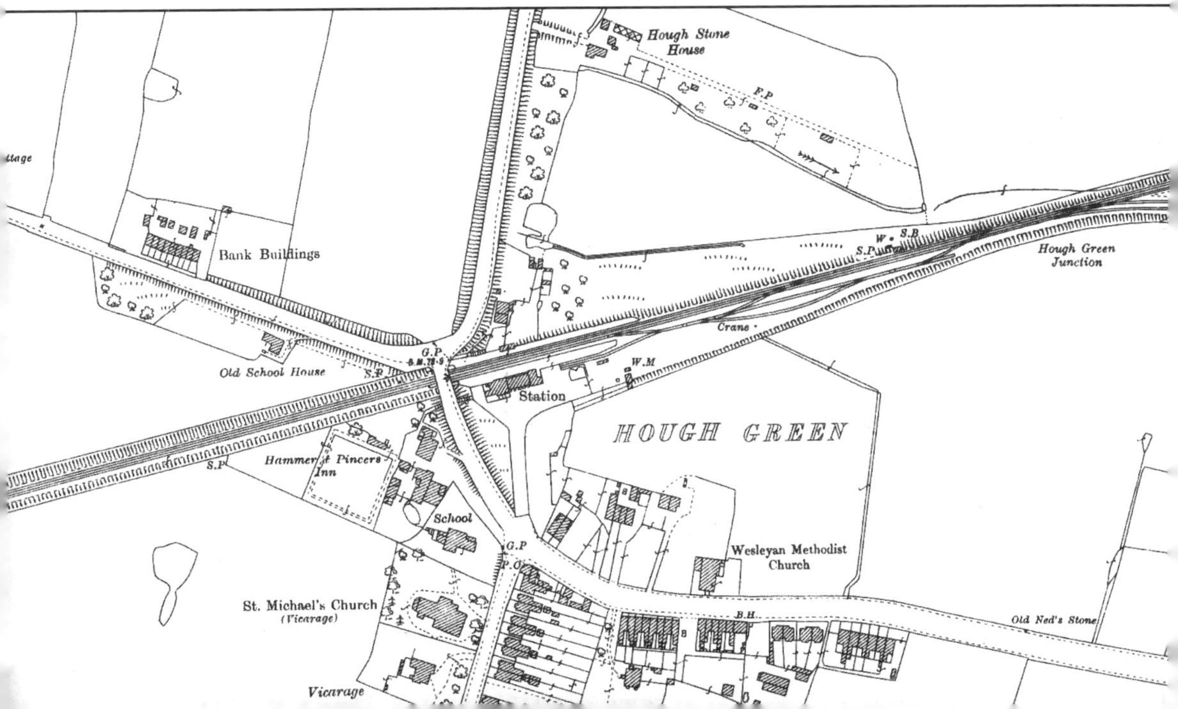

70. This eastward view dated from around 1930 and featured a Sentinel steam railcar calling with a down service. They were used regularly on stopping trains between Liverpool Central and both Stockport Tiviot Dale and Widnes Central. In the background was Hough Green Junction with the Widnes Central loop going off to the right, and the associated signal box on the up side which operated between 1879 and 1961. The full extent of the goods yard could be seen. (P. Laming coll.)

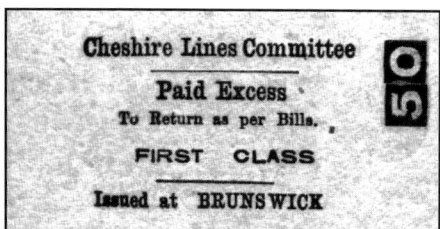

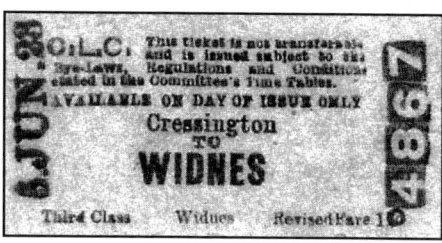

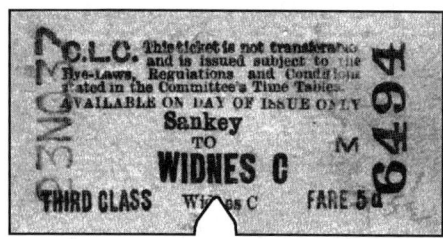

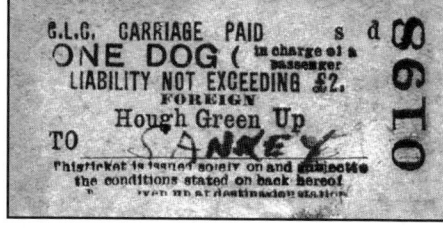

71. A similar view from 4th October 1986 saw class 108 DMU nos 54275 and 51421 pausing with the 13.43 Manchester Oxford Road – Hunts Cross. In the intervening time the platforms had been lengthened, the goods yard closed (from 1st June 1964), the Widnes Loop closed, and the signal box replaced. This box of LMR standard design was abolished on 18th December 1988. (T. Heavyside)

72. This westward view from 30th April 2007 recorded TPE DMU no. 185109 at speed with the 10.22 Liverpool – Scarborough. The original CLC buildings remained intact, whilst the line disappeared into the distance towards Halewood as straight as a die. (A. C. Hartless)

HALEWOOD

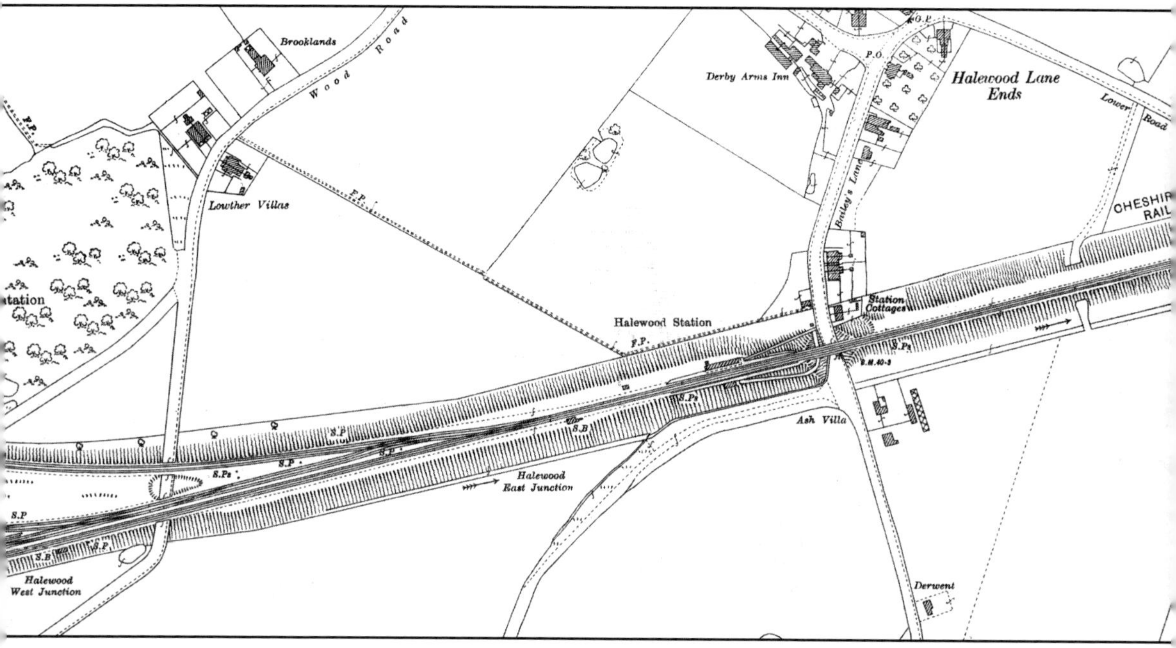

XVIII. Soon after leaving Hough Green the Borough of Halton is left behind and our route crosses into the Borough of Knowsley. Halewood was originally 2¼ miles from Hough Green and opened at the same time. It was located on an embankment and lightweight timber buildings were provided. There were no goods facilities. Halewood was a small village when the railway arrived and did not begin to grow until the 1950s, after the first station closed from 17th September 1951. Residential growth was such that a second station was opened ¼ mile west on 16th May 1988.

73. The Midland Railway ran its own services over the CLC to Liverpool from the east Midlands. Sometime around 1905, 4-2-2 no. 623 was seen approaching the station forging westward. There were 85 of these elegant Johnson singles built at Derby between 1887-99; the last was withdrawn in 1928. No. 673 of this class was preserved and in 2024 was at the National Railway Museum, York. (Disused-stations.org.uk)

74. This westward view pre-1914 captured an up express behind class 11A 4-4-0 no. 854 passing the main building, which was reached from ground level by an inclined driveway. The footbridge appeared on the map of 1907, but was subsequently replaced by a subway. (P. Laming coll.)

75. Looking west from the down platform class 13 4-2-2 no. 967 roared through with what was probably another Liverpool Central – Manchester Central express. The date was sometime between the locomotive's introduction in 1900 and the outbreak of WWI in 1914. At left was Halewood East Junction signal box. This dated from the opening of the CLC's North Liverpool line on 1st December 1879 and lasted until 21st October 1962 when it was replaced by an LMR box, which was abolished on 24th January 1982. It marked the start of quadruple track as far as Hunts Cross West Junction. A short distance further on was Halewood West Junction; the access to Halewood Sidings. (R. Humm coll.)

76. The second station was built between Hollies Road and the site of Halewood West Junction. This is how it appeared on 30th April 2007 as Northern DMU no. 150142 called with the 10.55 Liverpool – Manchester Oxford Road. The down platform had an identical shelter. There was a ticket office of similar red bricks on Hollies Road south of the railway bridge. The trees to the right of the train occupied the formation of the former goods lines. The site of Hunts Cross East Junction was immediately beyond the occupation bridge in the distance. (A.C. Hartless)

WEST OF HALEWOOD

77. In February 1959 class O4 2-8-0 no. 63613 was seen passing along the down goods line alongside the well-occupied Halewood Sidings. The loco was a Doncaster based engine at this date and, judging by its cleanliness, it might have been running-in after a visit to Gorton Works. The long-wheelbase wagons, comprising a very lengthy train, appeared to be carrying pipes, possibly for export. All this informs us how important a freight artery the CLC once was. (J. Peden/8D Association)

EAST OF HUNTS CROSS

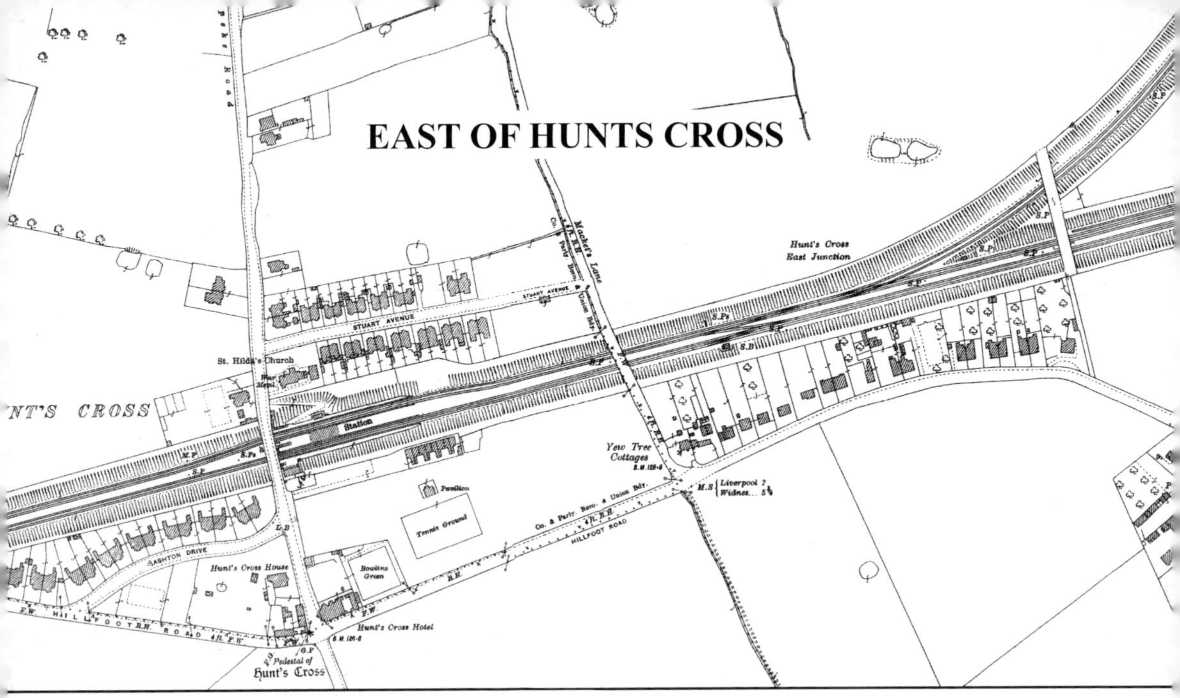

XIX. Mackets Lane, in the centre of the map, marks the boundary between Knowsley Borough and the City of Liverpool.

78. This was an eastward view from Mackets Lane bridge in April 1962. 5MT 4-6-0 no. 44964 (9E) was approaching with a service for Liverpool Central and had just passed Hunts Cross East Junction signal box. This dated from 1881 and was abolished from 21st October 1962. The lines branching left in the background were the west to north side of the Halewood triangle leading to the North Liverpool line. (J. Peden/8D Association)

0130
CYCLE CHECK LABEL
HALEWOOD Up
TO

Cheshire Lines Committee
ONE BICYCLE
accompanied by a passenger
AT CO'S RISK
FOR CONDITIONS SEE BACK
HALEWOOD Up
TO s d
This ticket which is available for a single journey only must be given up at destination station
0130

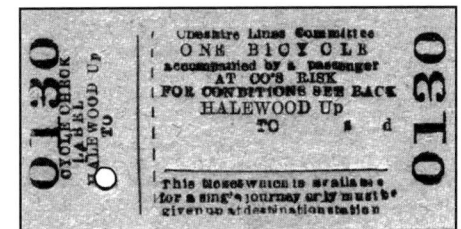

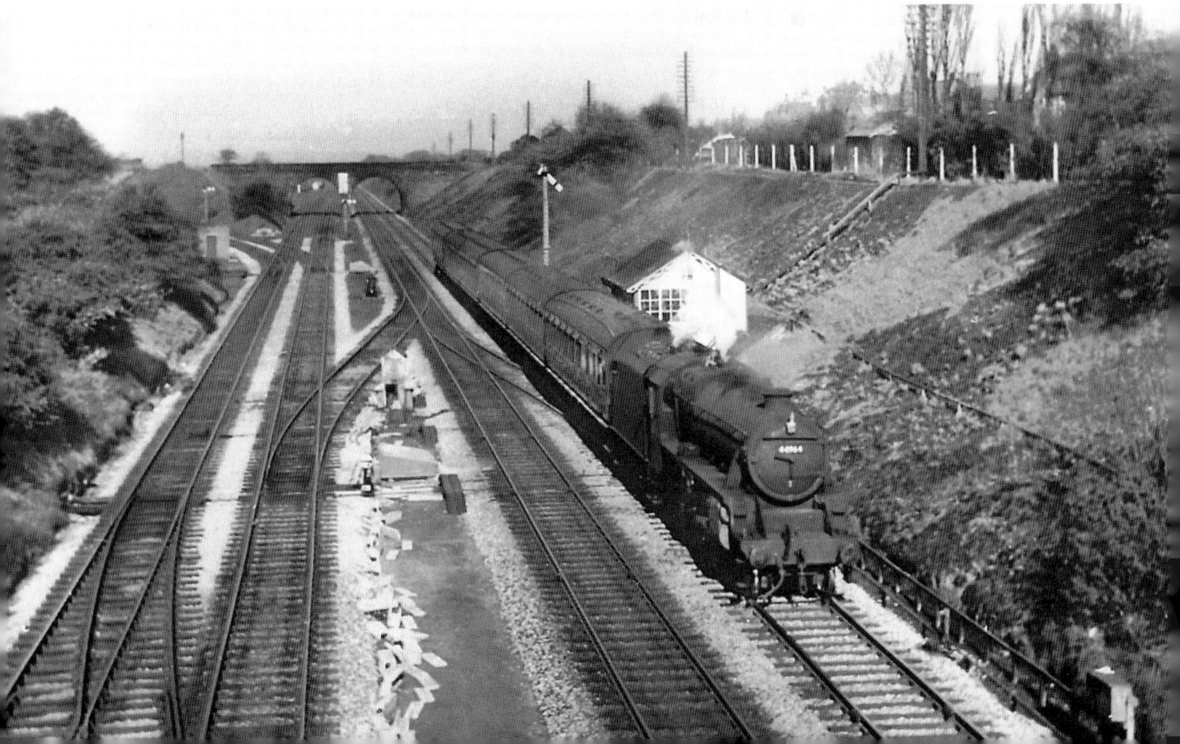

HUNTS CROSS

Hunts Cross supposedly takes its name from a long-established rural crossroads which was a rendezvous for the local hunt. It was 1¼ miles from the first Halewood station and is 7 miles from Liverpool of which it is an outer suburb. It was first in the timetable for May 1874; there were no goods facilities.

The station is in a cutting and the main building extended from platform level to the booking office at street level with the station master's house above. The number of platforms was augmented from two to four in 1883 when the line was quadrupled; the two new platforms generally handled services to/from Gateacre. This remained the basic layout until the withdrawal of the Gateacre trains from 17th April 1972 after which the two later lines were taken up. From 16th May 1983 the former down Gateacre line was reinstated as far as the station's east end when the 750 volts DC Merseyrail electric service was extended from Garston. Step-free access arrived on 29th September 2022 with the opening of a new footbridge with 16 person lifts.

79. This was a westward view from Mackets Lane bridge on 26th April 1965 as 4MT 2-6-4T no. 42455 (9E) departed Hunts Cross with the 7.42am Liverpool Central – Manchester Central. At right was a Derby twin-car DMU with the 8.00am to Gateacre. Note the immaculate state of the permanent way. The station, in the background, was little changed in appearance since 1883. The canopy on the central island did not extend as far as the bridge, which carried Speke Road. Close inspection showed the earlier half of the bridge on the left was a brick arch, but the later span to its right was a girder. (D. Pool/8D Association)

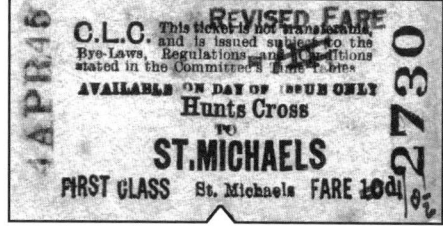

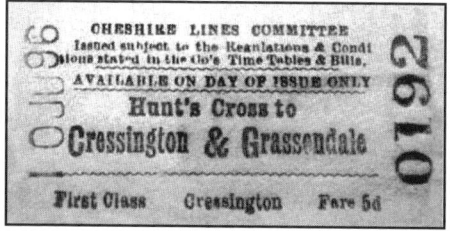

80. This picture was dated 30th May 1983, two weeks after the start of electric services from Liverpool Central Low Level. The view was east from the station footbridge. A pair of class 507 EMUs had just arrived at the terminal platform 3 on the left and some of its passengers were transferring to the waiting DMU at platform 2 for Warrington Central. This appeared to be a 3-car class 115 formation with two power cars sandwiching a trailer still in Rail Blue livery. These units, in 4-car sets, were introduced in 1960 as the first diesels in regular service on the CLC main line. The building beyond the station athwart the formation of the Gateacre lines was Hunts Cross Signalling Centre, which opened on 5th December 1982 and, in 2024, controlled the route eastwards beyond Widnes (Farnworth). (T. Heavyside)

81. On 10th September 1995 no. 47845 *County of Kent* was seen accelerating the diverted 13.26 Liverpool – London Paddington Inter-City service through platform 2. This was equipped with third rail for emergency use leading from the crossover beyond the bridge. Note the much-improved waiting room serving platforms 2 & 3. (D. Birmingham)

← *This street view dated from 20th March 2024. At left was the upper section of the original station building, now a pub-restaurant called The Waiting Room. To its right were the more modest modern booking facilities. (D. Birmingham)*

82. On 21st June 2023 TPE's no. 68025 *Superb* was seen working the 15.24 Cleethorpes – Liverpool. It had just passed beneath Speke Road bridge, behind which could be seen the recently constructed station lift shafts. Just visible in platform 3 was a Merseyrail class 507 EMU. (D. Birmingham)

WEST OF HUNTS CROSS
(including the Hunts Cross Chord)

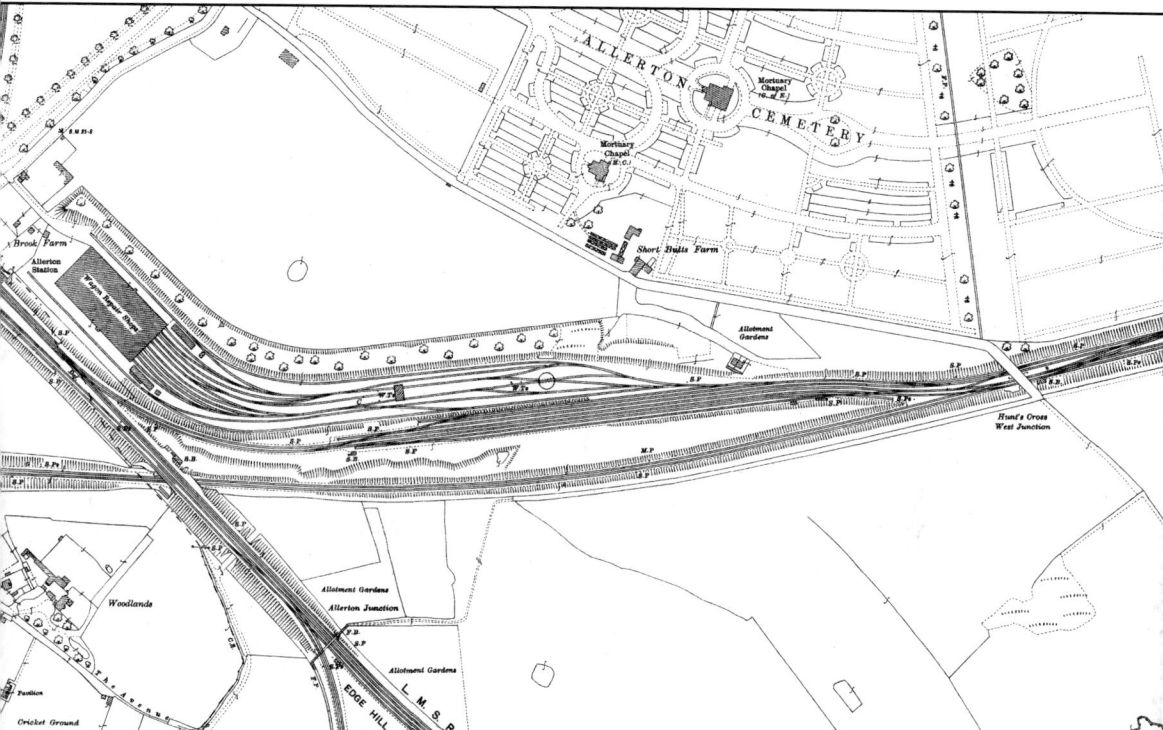

XX. Hunts Cross West Junction was created one mile west of the station on 14th May 1873 when the CLC opened a half mile goods link, the Hunts Cross Chord, to Allerton LNW. From here CLC trains had running powers to Wavertree LNW where a short branch led to the CLC's Wavertree and Edge Hill goods depot, which operated from 1st November 1864 until 3rd September 1973. It dealt inter alia with livestock imports.

The CLC opened Allerton loco shed on the north side of the Chord in 1882. It had 10 roads and was intended to replace the cramped Brunswick shed in the provision of locos for freight trains to/from Halewood yard. However, because no traffic originated or terminated at Allerton locos using the shed were required to travel light engine, which was wasteful on fuel, and by 1886 the depot had become a sub-shed of Brunswick. After 1897 it was used solely for carriage and wagon repairs. It stood until the early 1970s.

The shed yard was chosen as the site for a new Traction Maintenance Depot for diesel and electric trains when the Crewe – Liverpool electrification was planned. The five-road shed opened in 1960 initially to maintain the new class 115 DMUs that replaced steam on the CLC passenger services and, from 1961, the 25kV AC locos and AM4 EMUs for the Crewe trains. A wheel lathe was installed in a separate building c1981 which was accessible by the 750v DC Merseyrail units. The depot was mothballed between 2008-11 but was then refurbished. Three of the five shed roads were extended at the west end in 2017 to accommodate Northern's new CAF diesel and electric units.

The Hunts Cross Chord was realigned to accommodate the depot and became a passenger line from 5th September 1966 when the CLC main line services were transferred from Liverpool Central to Lime Street. After that date the only passenger service on the CLC route between Hunts Cross West Junction and Liverpool Central was between the latter and Gateacre. Freight traffic to and from Brunswick lingered until around 1977 when the line closed entirely whilst it was converted for operation solely by Merseyrail.

83. This was a westward view of Hunts Green West Junction with 4MT 2-6-4T no. 42664 hauling a Liverpool Central – Manchester Central service. It probably dates from the period between May 1952 and July 1954 when the loco was allocated to Brunswick, its only posting to the CLC. The Hunts Cross Chord diverged to the right and on either side of it were carriage sidings with rakes of stock. Hunts Cross West Junction signal box was behind the photographer on the down side. There were three generations of boxes here, the first dating from the opening of the line until quadrupling in 1883, the second thence until December 1956, and the third, another flat-roofed LMR type located in the vee of the junction, until December 1982 when it was replaced by Hunts Cross Signalling Centre. All the tracks in this picture received overhead electrification in 1961, enabling shunt moves in and around Allerton depot. This was reported being dismantled in August 2023. (R. Stephens/8D Association)

84. This LMR Press Office picture of the newly electrified railway was entitled 'Servicing electric locomotives at Allerton District Electric Depot'. The cleanliness of the shed floor could be compared with the dirt of a steam shed showing that BR was wise to segregate the new forms of power. The contemporary working practices, with an un-chocked ladder supported only by the locomotive, were still steam-age however. There were four light blue electric locos in this eastward view, of which the nearest, type AL5 no. E3063 (later no. 85008), was delivered from Doncaster Works in October 1961 and had scarcely got its buffers dirty. (BR/R Humm coll.)

85. An open day was held at the depot on 26th July 1969 centred on the CLC shed. Three steam locomotives were hauled from Tyseley for the event and took turns hauling a carriage 100 yards up and down the shed yard. The photographer caught LMS Jubilee no. 5593 *Kolhapur* and GW Castle no. 7029 *Clun Castle* between trips; the third loco was LMS 5MT no. 5428. Behind *Clun Castle* was an AL6 (later class 86) electric loco on display taking a break from hauling Liverpool to London Euston expresses. The CLC shed formed the right-hand background with the roof of the three-road west bay above *Clun Castle*, the four-road centre bay above its coach and a glimpse of the east bay above the AL6. The strong arm of the law was keeping watch over proceedings. (D. Pool/8D Association)

86. This was the east end of the new shed on 28th December 1983. Visible at left were two of six open-air stabling sidings, one of which was holding a visiting class 110 DMU. The three and two road sheds were in the centre, and at right a siding held two class 08 shunters flanking no. 40033 *Empress of England*. (A.C. Hartless)

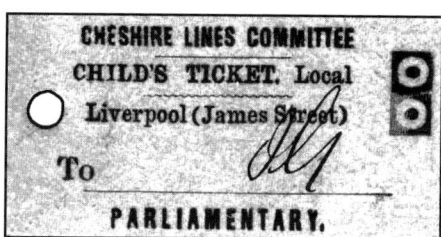

LIVERPOOL SOUTH PARKWAY

Liverpool South Parkway opened on 11th June 2006 when its low level platforms 5 and 6 replaced Garston, which was 250 yards further west. Platforms 1-4 comprised the former Allerton station on the ex-LNW Lime Street – Runcorn line. The two elements of the enlarged station were linked by a covered footway leading to a shared concourse and bus terminal. Further pictures can be found in *Liverpool to Runcorn*.

87. On 29th April 2014, Merseyrail EMU no. 507029 ran in with the 11.21 Hunts Cross – Southport. Note the heavily engineered footbridge and the wide stairways. The bridge carrying the former LNW line was visible in the background. (A.C. Hartless)

GARSTON

XXI. Garston opened on 1st April 1874 1⅝ miles from Hunts Cross where the CLC line was crossed by Woolton Road. The goods station was at Garston Dock, terminus of the Garston & Liverpool Railway, although there was a horse dock at the passenger station at the west end on the down side. The station closed with the withdrawal of the Liverpool Central – Gateacre service, but re-opened as Garston (Merseyside), to distinguish it from Garston (Herts), from 2nd January 1978 when it became the southern terminus of Merseyrail's Northern Line from Southport via Liverpool Central Low Level. This route was extended to Hunts Cross on 16th May 1983 and the station was closed from 11th June 2006 when Liverpool South Parkway replaced it.

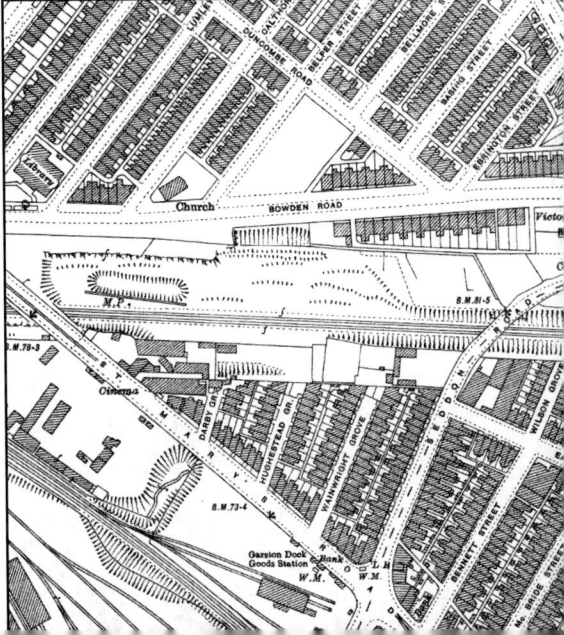

88. This was an eastward view from the first decade of the 20th century. At left with a rake of suburban passenger stock was the up platform loop used to reverse short workings from Liverpool Central. The gaslights were an early pattern which pre-dated the introduction of gas mantles. Woolton Road bridge was behind the footbridge with The Avenue beyond. Woolton Road was widened in the 1930s when the no. 33 tram from Pier Head terminated here. When Horrocks Avenue was built after WWII its junction with Woolton Road spanned the railway and created a 62-yard tunnel. The Avenue was replaced by high density housing and its bridge was demolished. (P. Laming coll.)

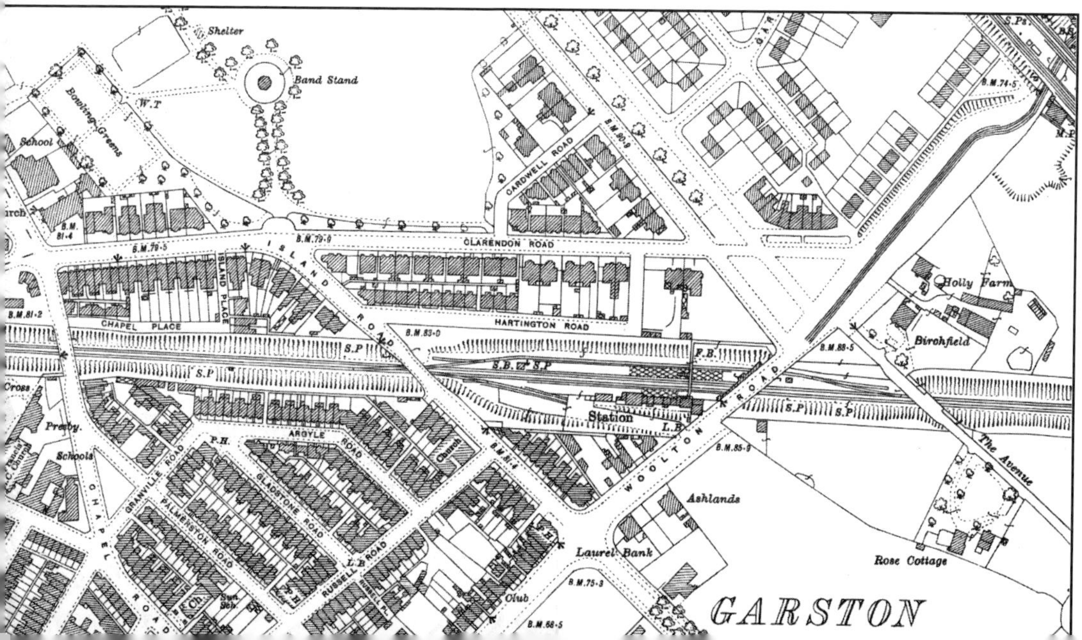

89. This picture captured Fowler 4MT 2-6-4T no. 42352 approaching Garston from Liverpool Central. It was undated, but the loco was on Brunswick's allocation from April 1953 until July 1959. Garston Station signal box opened soon after the line. It received a new 20 lever frame in 1903 and was abolished in July 1967. The up passenger loop was lifted sometime before the closure of the signal box. (R. Stephens/8D Association)

90. This was another eastward view, taken during the closure period between April 1972 and the coming of Merseyrail. Other than the loss of the footbridge canopy the structures were little changed from picture 88. The down platform had an interesting array of buildings. The furthest from the camera, with the bold finials, contained the ticket office at street level and steps down to the platform. The building in the centre with its three dormers was the station house and the one closest to the photographer was originally a waiting room. (D. Birmingham coll.)

91. When the station reopened only the former down line was used until the service was extended to Hunts Cross. LMS designed class 503 EMUs worked the line until new trains became available. One of the 1956 batch of the latter had just arrived on 10th March 1979. A road had been built at right serving a new station entrance/ticket office/waiting room. The up side canopy, footbridge, and CLC entrance building had all been demolished. (E.V. Richards)

92. The first new trains mentioned above were the 33 class 507 EMUs which were delivered in 1978-79 and still served Merseyrail at the start of 2023. On 5th June 2005 no. 507020 was seen arriving with a Hunts Cross – Southport service. The station house had survived but would soon be flattened. The new building seen in the previous picture had been extended and a canopy added, making for an uncomfortably narrow platform. A small shelter had been provided on the outbound platform. Immediately behind the photographer was a gently-graded ramped covered footbridge built circa 1983. To the rear of the train could be seen the down platform of the emerging Liverpool South Parkway. (A.C. Hartless)

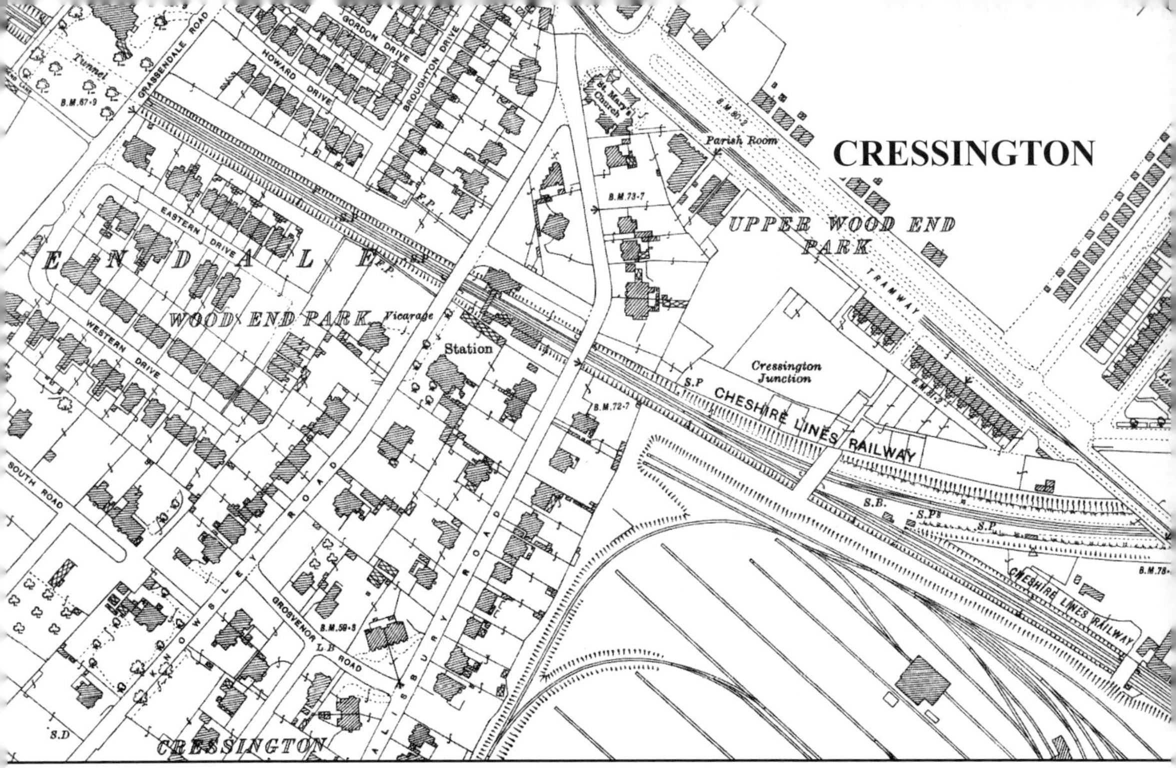

CRESSINGTON

XXII. Cressington station was ¾ mile west of Garston. Cressington Junction was six chains before the station. Here the CLC main line from Manchester trailed into the Garston & Liverpool. This opened on 1st June 1864 from an end-on junction with the LNW immediately west of its Garston Dock station that had opened on 1st July 1852 (see *Liverpool to Runcorn*). The distance from Garston Dock to Cressington was only 34 chains and incorporated Garston Central goods station (map XXI) which lasted until 7th September 1964. There were no timetabled passenger trains on this section after the opening of the CLC main line, and it closed entirely from 15th August 1977.

93. This was Cressington Junction in around 1974 as no. 47006 took a Freightliner from Garston FLT to Trafford Park. It had already travelled along the G&L at the left of the picture and visited Brunswick for the loco to run round. The signal box was originally of normal height. It was abolished from 4th September 1977. (D. Lennon)

94. Cressington was known as Cressington & Grassendale from 1877 until its temporary closure in 1972. Merseyrail shortened it to simply Cressington. This was a well-to-do area when the line first opened, which was reflected in the station's architecture. This survived into the BR era, and thankfully it was extensively restored during the closure. There were no goods facilities. Here it was seen on 3rd July 1986 as EMU no. 508141 led the 11.30 Southport – Hunts Cross. The footbridge connected the street level booking office with the down platform. The 41 class 508s were contemporaneous with the 507s but built for the southwest London commuter routes as 4-coach sets. By 1986 they had all migrated to Merseyside, but each set left one of its central trailers behind as Merseyrail could only accommodate a maximum of six car trains, i.e. 2x3. (T. Heavyside)

AIGBURTH (formerly MERSEY ROAD)

XXIII. This was known as Mersey Road until 1880, Mersey Road & Aigburth until it temporarily closed from 17th April 1972, and Aigburth when it reopened on 2nd January 1978. It was ¾ mile from Cressington and there were no goods facilities.

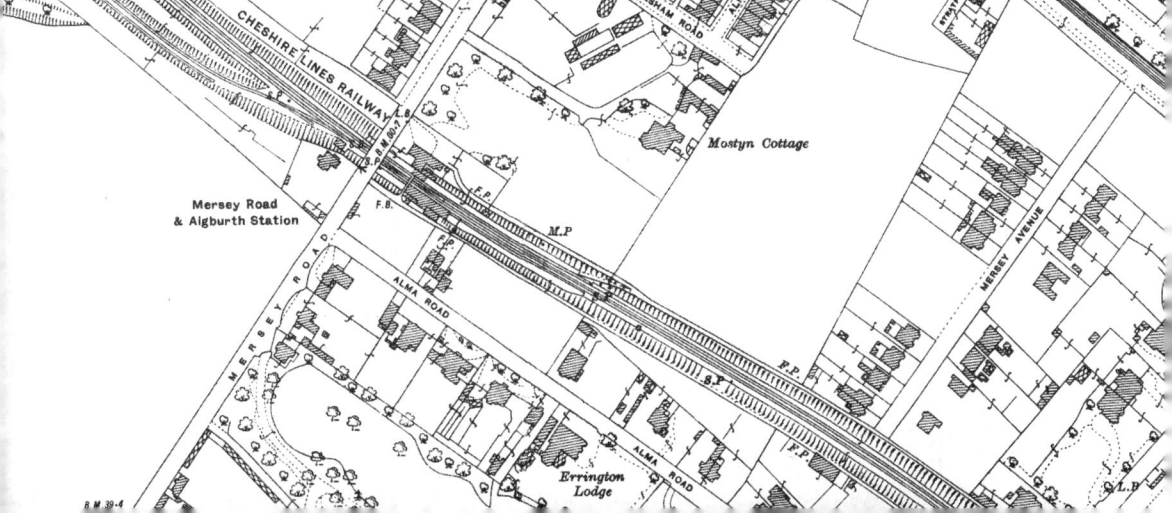

95. The main building was photographed on 30th November 2013. Like Cressington it survived the closure period, during which it was renovated. Much of the G&L was built in a shallow cutting and as at Cressington the ticket office was at street level with a footbridge leading therefrom to the opposite platform. In June 2024 it was announced that lifts were going to be installed here to provide step-free access to both platforms. (E. Pollock)

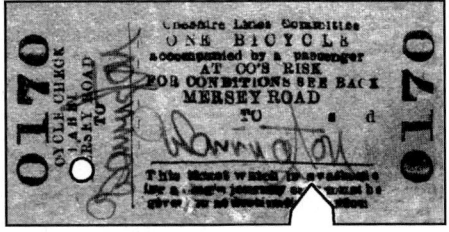

96. On 7th August 2015 no. 508137 led the 11.42 Southport – Hunts Cross affording a view of the down side building. (D. Birmingham)

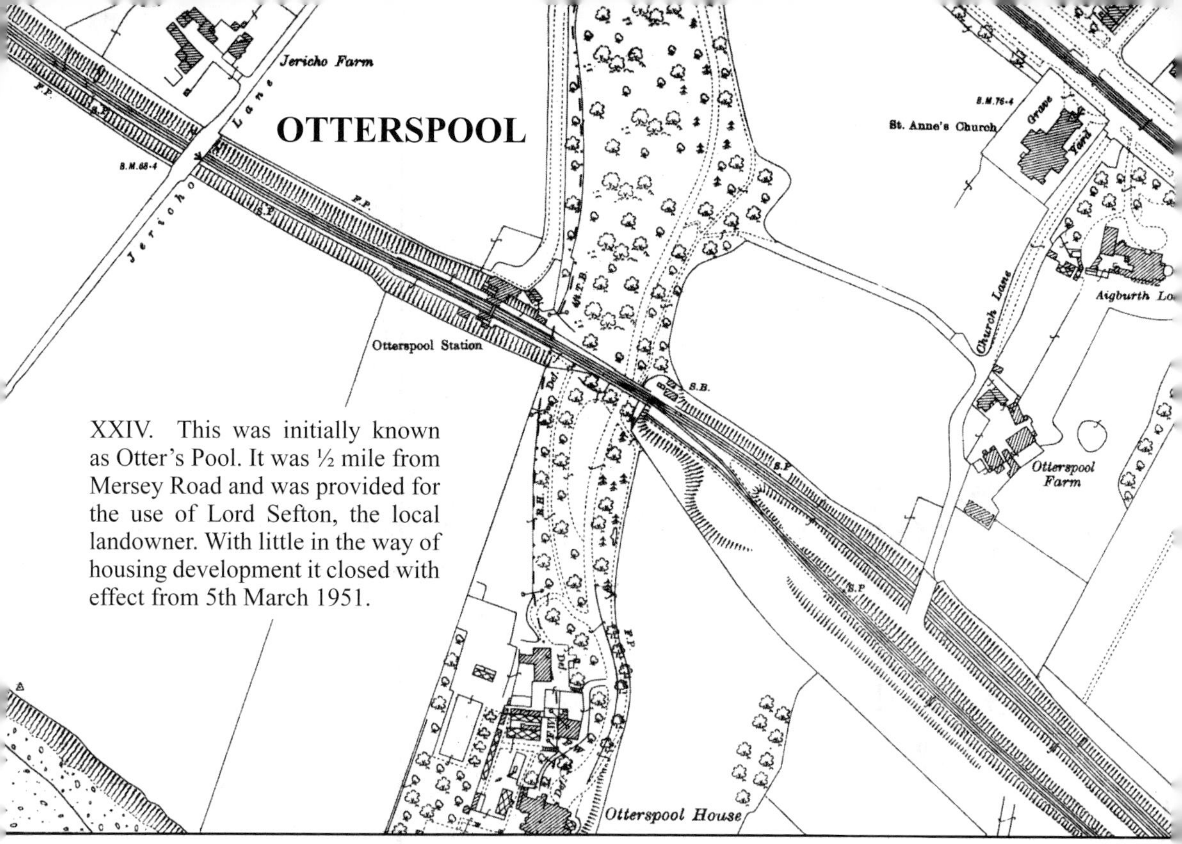

OTTERSPOOL

XXIV. This was initially known as Otter's Pool. It was ½ mile from Mersey Road and was provided for the use of Lord Sefton, the local landowner. With little in the way of housing development it closed with effect from 5th March 1951.

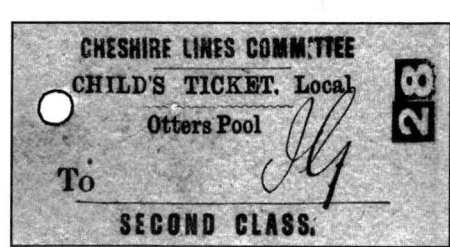

97. This eastward view dated from circa 1930. The main building bore a striking resemblance to Mersey Road. The signal box was on the up side just beyond the station and its gable roof could be discerned above the right-hand end of the footbridge. It was the second box at Otterspool and had 36 levers. It operated from September 1912 when a loop line opened from Mersey Road. This was built to serve a proposed new coal dock on the Mersey but the plan was abandoned in 1913. The loop was useful for staging freight traffic and it was retained until the early 1970s by which time it had become a repository for redundant wagons. The box was abolished on 12th December 1973. (J. Mann coll./Disused-stations.org.uk)

ST. MICHAEL'S

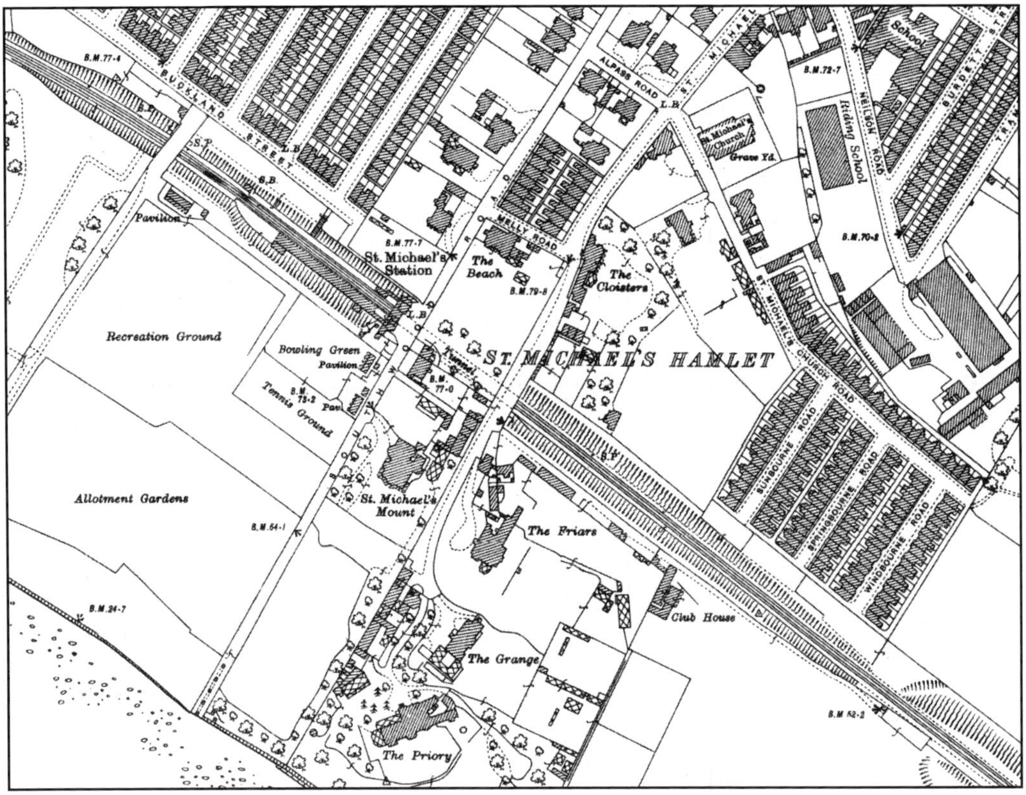

XXV. This was a little under one mile from Otterspool, which included the 200 yards of Fulwood Tunnel. The district takes its name from the church of St. Michael-in-the-Hamlet, Aigburth, which took from 1813 to 1900 to complete and was notable for using cast iron as a significant component in its construction.

98. This was a postcard view of the exterior in the Edwardian era. There is an affinity with the MS&L designed stations further east on the CLC main line, but here the building is at right angles to the tracks.
(P. Laming coll.)

99. Closure appeared imminent when the platform structures were recorded on 31st August 1966, but the Gateacre service clung on for almost six more years. Note the 103 yards St.Michael's Tunnel, and the steep stairs leading from the booking office to the down platform. (H.B. Priestley/R. Humm coll.)

← 100A. The National Gardens Festival was held nearby on a site reclaimed from the Mersey Estuary in 1984. The most obvious improvement to the station was the construction of two ramps to augment the original narrow staircases. These were in the background as no. 508123 arrived with the 13.35 Southport – Hunts Cross on 26th February 1988. (D. Birmingham)

→ 100B. In 2023 the ramps were replaced by lifts and new staircases. This was done tastefully so that the liftshafts blended in with the 1864 station building. On 8th June 2023 no. 507026 worked the 14.57 Southport – Hunts Cross. This unit was withdrawn soon afterwards and was scrapped at Sims yard, Newport Docks in September 2023. The design on the side was part of the contemporary Merseyrail livery. (D. Birmingham)

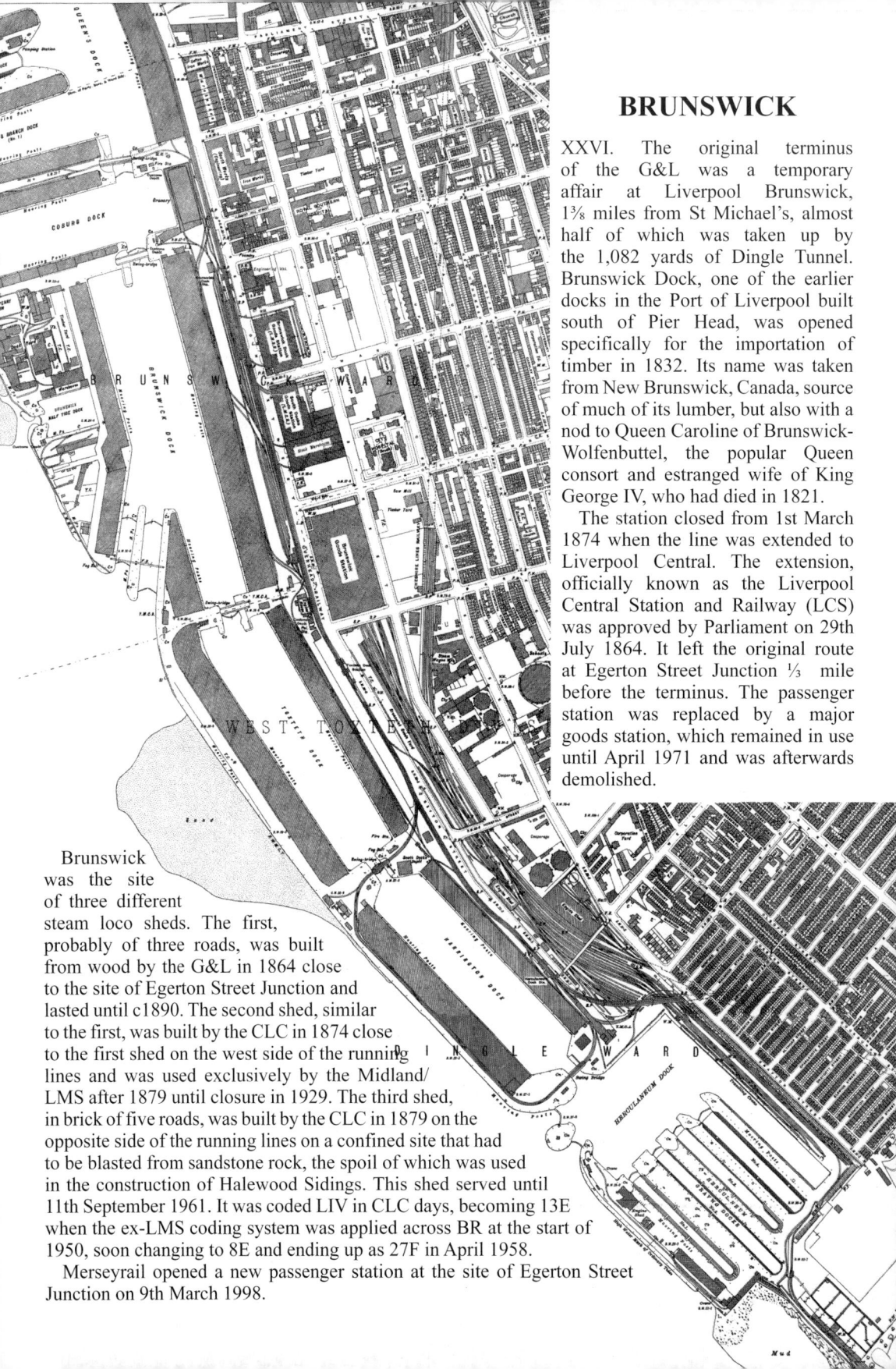

BRUNSWICK

XXVI. The original terminus of the G&L was a temporary affair at Liverpool Brunswick, 1⅜ miles from St Michael's, almost half of which was taken up by the 1,082 yards of Dingle Tunnel. Brunswick Dock, one of the earlier docks in the Port of Liverpool built south of Pier Head, was opened specifically for the importation of timber in 1832. Its name was taken from New Brunswick, Canada, source of much of its lumber, but also with a nod to Queen Caroline of Brunswick-Wolfenbuttel, the popular Queen consort and estranged wife of King George IV, who had died in 1821.

The station closed from 1st March 1874 when the line was extended to Liverpool Central. The extension, officially known as the Liverpool Central Station and Railway (LCS) was approved by Parliament on 29th July 1864. It left the original route at Egerton Street Junction ⅓ mile before the terminus. The passenger station was replaced by a major goods station, which remained in use until April 1971 and was afterwards demolished.

Brunswick was the site of three different steam loco sheds. The first, probably of three roads, was built from wood by the G&L in 1864 close to the site of Egerton Street Junction and lasted until c1890. The second shed, similar to the first, was built by the CLC in 1874 close to the first shed on the west side of the running lines and was used exclusively by the Midland/LMS after 1879 until closure in 1929. The third shed, in brick of five roads, was built by the CLC in 1879 on the opposite side of the running lines on a confined site that had to be blasted from sandstone rock, the spoil of which was used in the construction of Halewood Sidings. This shed served until 11th September 1961. It was coded LIV in CLC days, becoming 13E when the ex-LMS coding system was applied across BR at the start of 1950, soon changing to 8E and ending up as 27F in April 1958.

Merseyrail opened a new passenger station at the site of Egerton Street Junction on 9th March 1998.

101. This was a northward view of the new loco shed in around 1902. Like the contemporary picture (no. 18) of Trafford Park the depot was neat and tidy, a credit to all involved. The line up of locomotives comprised from left to right: class 13 4-2-2 no. 968, class 9G (LNE F2) 2-4-2T no. 782, and class 11A 4-4-0s nos 268 and 878. No. 268 was the first of its class and went into traffic in September 1897. No. 782 was new in April 1898 and 878 in March 1899; both were built by Beyer Peacock. The single wheeler was the newest, delivered in May 1900. (W. Hulme)

102. This south eastward view of circa 1932 was taken from the footbridge seen in the previous image linking Grafton Street with the Herculaneum Dock station of the Liverpool Overhead Railway (LOR), which opened in 1893 and closed at the end of 1956. The two locomotives were standing on the southernmost track of the shed yard; this housed the shear legs heavy lifting tackle. LNE class B7 no. 5078 was a GC class 9Q mixed traffic 4-6-0 built at Gorton in 1921, whilst no. 5853 was a GC class 11A. The signal box was Brunswick South, a Saxby & Farmer installation of 1878 that was abolished on 20th September 1936 when electric colour lights replaced semaphores. The two running lines disappeared into Dingle Trunnel. Behind the signal box two lines led through gates into the Herculaneum Dock estate. Above them was the girder bridge carrying the LOR into its tunnel through the sandstone to its Dingle terminus. The clearance between the CLC and LOR tunnels was said to have been less than 3 feet. (A.G. Ellis/R. Humm coll.)

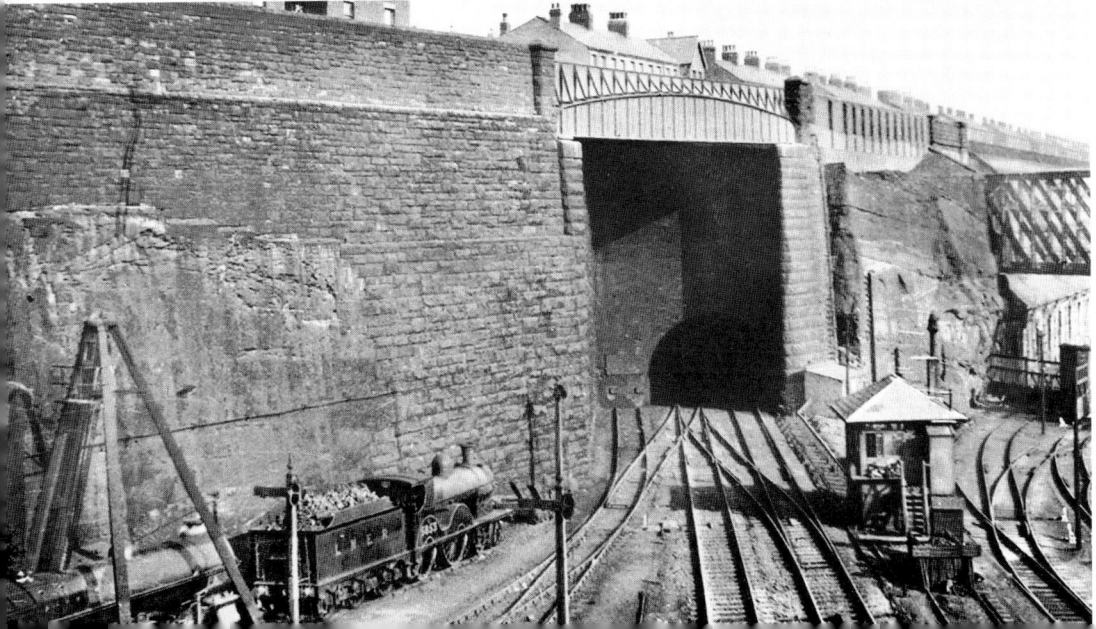

103. This atmospheric steam shed scene was recorded on 21st April 1950. Four of the shed's five roads could be seen on the left side of the picture. The three locos on view appeared to be an N5 (GC class 9F) 0-6-2T, an LMS 4F 0-6-0 and a D11 Improved Director (GC class 11F) 4-4-0. Much of the shed roof was missing in the aftermath of WWII until it was refurbished in about 1955. To the right of the running shed were the coaling roads, with an unidentifiable locomotive, beyond which was a 60-foot turntable. At right was another N5, no. 69272. This was a resident from February 1949 until withdrawal in April 1956. Note the steps, on which were three men and a bike, linking Grafton Street and the shed. The gasworks added their odour to the coal smoke, warm oil and steam of the loco shed. (H.C. Casserley/R. Humm coll.)

104. The G&L's passenger terminus was a temporary timber structure that stood in the vicinity of this Italianate three-storey building, the goods offices, on the corner of Sefton Street and Northumberland Street, 1¼ miles from Pier Head. The massive goods warehouse stood alongside it and was seen some time in the late 1960s. (P. Hanson coll.)

105. This early evening view was taken in April 1968 in the last weeks of everyday steam in Liverpool, which ended officially on 5th May, from the same bridge as picture 102 but looking north. A 9F 2-10-0 was running light engine to the former LNW Speke Junction shed, that took over some of the duties of Brunswick when it closed, whilst a class 5MT and van were proceeding to Brunswick Yard for their next turn. The eagle-eyed might also spot a Yorkshire Engine 0-4-0 diesel shunter, later TOPS class 02, of which 20 were built in 1960 to replace short wheelbase steam shunters in places such as the Liverpool docks. In the background were the cranes of Brunswick Dock, Brunswick North signal box (opened in 1904 and abolished on 12th December 1973 when Brunswick yard closed), Brunswick Goods warehouse and Egerton Street Junction. (P.H. Hanson)

106. This was a northward view of the new station on 25th October 1999 as no. 508114 departed with the 14.51 Hunts Cross – Southport. The station had the appearance of a mass of steel with ramped walkways in all directions. The unit was about to pass beneath Caryl Street whilst one of the towers of the distant Liver Building was visible between the train and the footbridge. (A.C. Hartless)

ST. JAMES

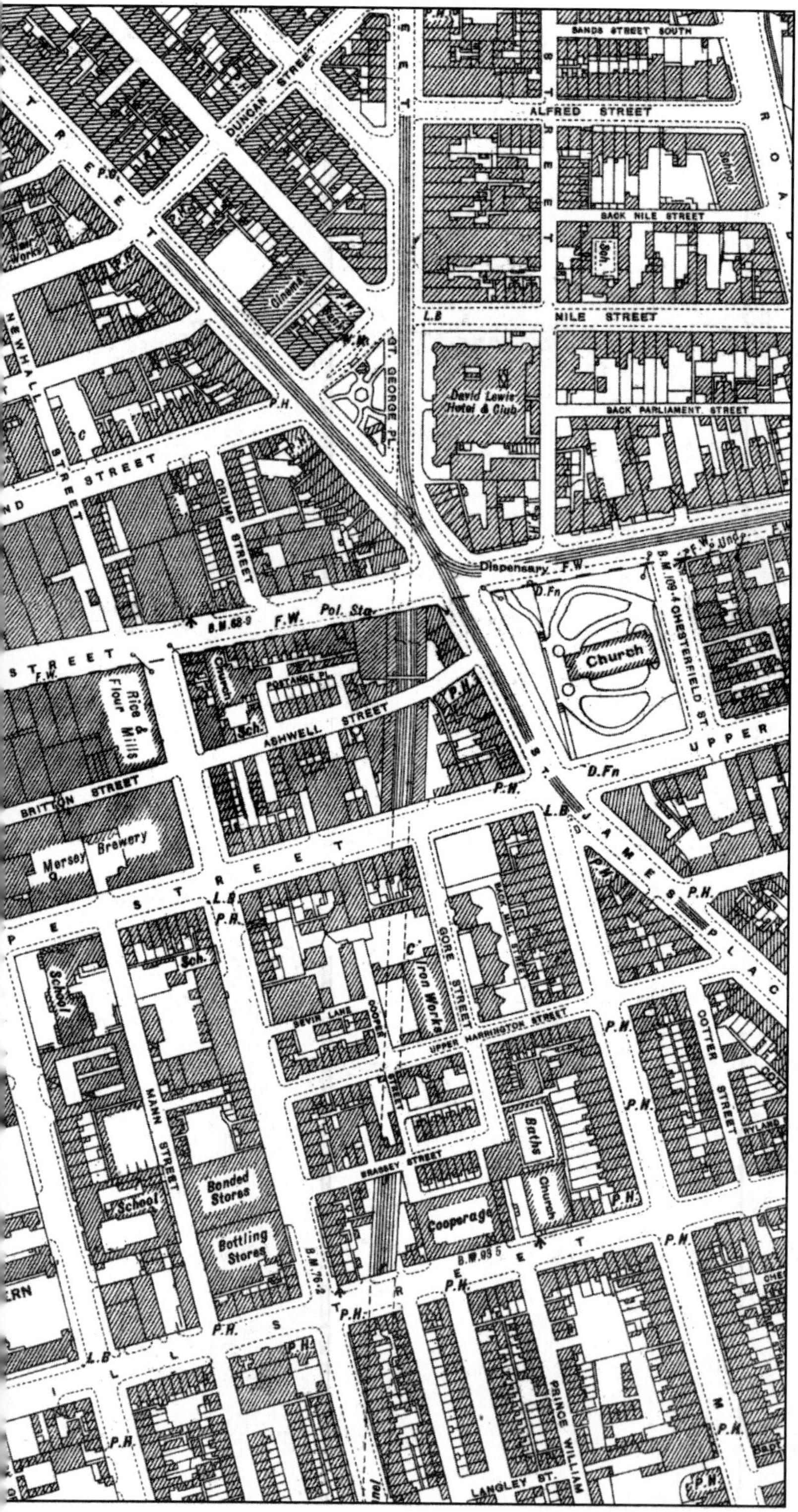

➔ 107. This was a northward view taken soon after the installation of colour light signalling between Liverpool Central and Brunswick in 1934, one of the earliest such schemes in the UK. There were three running lines, the middle one being generally used for light engine and empty stock moves. The bridge carried Parliament Street and was succeeded by Great George Street Tunnel. On 15th October 1913 the station was the scene of the worst accident on the CLC main line when an up express ran into the back of another that had made an emergency stop. Seven lives were lost. (D. Ibbotson)

← XXVII. There was one intermediate station, St James, on the LCS which was ¾ mile from Egerton Street Junction. It was preceded by four tunnels totalling 721 yards. It was open to air but below ground level and was crossed by three road bridges, including Ashwell Street. There were no goods facilities. The station closed as a wartime economy measure from 1st January 1917 but never reopened, until in 2014 plans were announced to rebuild it and funding was eventually confirmed. In April 2022 the new name Liverpool Baltic was chosen by public ballot. In late 2023 work was expected to start in 2025, with a prospective opening in 2028.

LIVERPOOL CENTRAL

108. This postcard from circa 1907 looked up Ranelagh Street, along which two trams were approaching, from its junction with Church Street. The station took up the central background, with its porte cochere just discernible. The font for the CENTRAL STATION sign was Art Nouveau, a reference perhaps to the Paris Metro, which Sir Edward Watkin would have known. The single-floor building partially obscured by the leading tram was the parcels office, and was the only structure to survive demolition; with the addition of an upper floor it still stood in 2024 as a retail unit. The prominent building beyond the station was Lewis's department store. (R. Humm coll.)

XXVIII. Liverpool Central was a further ¾ mile from St James. This stretch was almost entirely in tunnel, much of it beneath Great George Street, to the east of which, on St James's Mount, stands Liverpool Cathedral, built between 1904-78.

The station occupied a site of 5½ acres, some of which was formerly a timber yard but also required the demolition of residential and commercial property, for example, the Waterloo Hotel. The station was largely covered by a 164 feet single-span arched roof with a maximum height of 65 feet and comprised six passenger platforms, facilities for horses, milk and parcels, and a cab road. The terminal building was of three storeys and housed the headquarter offices of the CLC. It was all demolished in 1972. The forecourt, station building and concourse made way for a shopping centre.

109. This was the interior of the station on Saturday 6th April 1946. On the right, passengers were joining an express at platform 1, which appeared to be formed of LNE teak stock. The cab road separated platforms 1 and 2. Note the carriage siding between platforms 2 and 3. The notice on platforms 3 and 4 read MANCHESTER PASSENGERS ONLY BEYOND THIS POINT. At the upper left hand margin a locomotive could just be seen at the head of a train in platform 5. The overall roof extended only as far as the Newington bridge, beyond which there was a canopy over the cab road. (Stewart Bale Ltd/R Humm coll.)

110. On 21st April 1950, no. 62659 *Worsley-Taylor* made an energetic departure from platform 3 with the 7.30pm to Manchester Central. This was the last of 10 4-4-0s built by the GC in 1913 as class 11E 'Director', reclassified as D10 by the LNE. It was withdrawn in November 1954. Henry Wilson Worsley-Taylor (1847-1924) was a Director of the GC between 1901-22. He held the Recordership of Preston in the 1890s and was Conservative MP for Blackpool between 1901-05. He was son-in-law to Sir Edward Watkin and was created a Baronet in 1917. (H.C. Casserley/Disused-stations.com.)

111. By October 1959, former LMS designs had replaced Great Central locos. Here, 4MT 2-6-4T no. 42466 was standing at the buffer stops of platform 2 at 4.19pm and gave us a view of the terminal buildings and concourse. The shiny three-wheeled car was an invalid carriage. (H.C. Casserley/Disused-stations.com.)

112. After the diversion to Lime Street of all but the hourly Gateacre service in 1966 the station was rapidly wound down. By the time of this photograph, taken on 18th February 1967, the tracks had been removed from platforms 1-3 and the wide platform 1 & 2 had been given over to car parking. By the time of the last trains on 15th April 1972 the only track remaining was just enough to accommodate a 2-car DMU at the country end of platform 4, and demolition was already in progress.

The loco in the picture was 2MT 2-6-0 no. 46520, from Northwich, running round the stock of the Liverpool & Warrington Area Rail Tour in platform 4. This had the unusual aim of visiting the district's remaining steam sheds by steam train. To its rear could be seen the servicing yard, which had a turntable and refuelling facilities. The running lines towards St James disappeared beneath the girder bridge into Great George Street Tunnel. Liverpool Central signal box was the second box at the site and served from 1889-1972. It had an 88-lever frame, of which only six were in use by the end. (D. Lennon)

LIVERPOOL CENTRAL (LOW LEVEL)

Liverpool Central Low Level, the former Mersey Railway terminus, continued until 1975 when it closed for major works. The route to the Mersey Rail Tunnel was disconnected and replaced by a new double-track north to south cross-city link through a tunnel 1 mile 1,172 yards long between Sandhills and St James, connecting the former Lancashire & Yorkshire Railway's routes to Liverpool Exchange with the CLC line. This created Merseyrail's Northern Line from Southport, which opened to Liverpool Central on 2nd May 1977 and was extended to Garston on 2nd January 1978. (Electric services from Liverpool Exchange to Southport had commenced as early as 1904.) The CLC first conceived the idea of a cross-city tunnel in 1888 to link its South Liverpool line with its North Liverpool line at Huskisson but abandoned it as being too expensive. However, the Mersey Railway's sub-surface station was deliberately aligned with the CLC's Great George Street tunnel to facilitate a future link-up, 85 years later as it happened.

On 9th May 1977 a new single track clockwise loop line, all in tunnel, was opened beneath Liverpool city centre to carry services from the Mersey Rail Tunnel to Moorfields (which replaced Exchange and was also served by the Northern Line), Lime Street, and a deep-level platform at Central, thence back to the Wirral.

The station is one of the busiest in the UK outside London with 16.5m passengers recorded in 2019-20.

113. The scale of the vault beneath the main line station could be readily appreciated on 2nd September 1974 as a class 503 EMU awaited departure with a service for the Wirral. These units represented the third generation of power on the former Mersey Railway. Steam locomotives with special condensing apparatus were used until 1903. Their replacements were amongst the earliest electric trains in Britain, rated at 600V DC. They were supplemented in 1938 when the LMS electrified the former Wirral Railway lines to West Kirkby and New Brighton (see *Birkenhead to West Kirby*) and built new passenger stock that survived long enough to become TOPS class 503. A second batch of these built in 1956 replaced the last of the 1903 stock. (K. Lane)

114. The low-level platforms were closed from 28th July 1975 until 2nd May 1977 whilst the Link Line was under construction, and the opportunity was taken to refurbish them, resulting in a brighter and less cluttered environment. As noted earlier the class 503 units were replaced by class 507 and 508 sets, which were built at York between 1978 and 1980. These provided all Merseyrail services until 2023 when 53 new class 777 units, ordered in 2016 and built by Stadler in Switzerland, began to take over. Old and new were seen at Liverpool Central on 5th June 2023. At left, no. 777008 was waiting to work the 12.46 to Ormskirk whilst at platform 1 no. 507017 was arriving with the 11.57 Southport – Hunts Cross. Class 777 units were first used on the Southport – Hunts Cross service on 11th December 2023. (D. Birmingham)

2. Widnes Central Loop

The Widnes Central loop began in 1873 as a local initiative for a three-mile goods branch, the Widnes Railway, from Widnes East Junction (west of Sankey for Penketh) to Widnes to break the LNW's monopoly on the town's lucrative freight business. The following year the sponsor was dissolved and the MS&L took over the project. In 1875 the concern was transferred to the Sheffield & Midland Committee, a joint venture of the MS&L and the Midland Railway. The branch opened on 3rd April 1877. In 1878 the S&M took control of another local venture, the Widnes West Railway, linking the Widnes Railway with the CLC at Hough Green. and which included branches to Widnes West Bank and Ditton, home to numerous factories. It opened to goods on 1st July 1879, and a passenger service around the loop began on 1st August 1879. This last ran on 3rd October 1964. The loop closed completely from 6th December 1964 and was promptly lifted.

TANHOUSE LANE

XXIX. After leaving the CLC mainline at Widnes East Junction the Widnes Central loop soon reached the short-lived Widnes South Junction. Part of the north to south straight that followed was recycled to accommodate a section of the Fiddlers Ferry Power Station loop when that was built circa 1967.

Tanhouse Lane opened to passengers on 1st September 1890 to help workers reach the eastward spread of industry. It was 3¾ miles from Sankey.

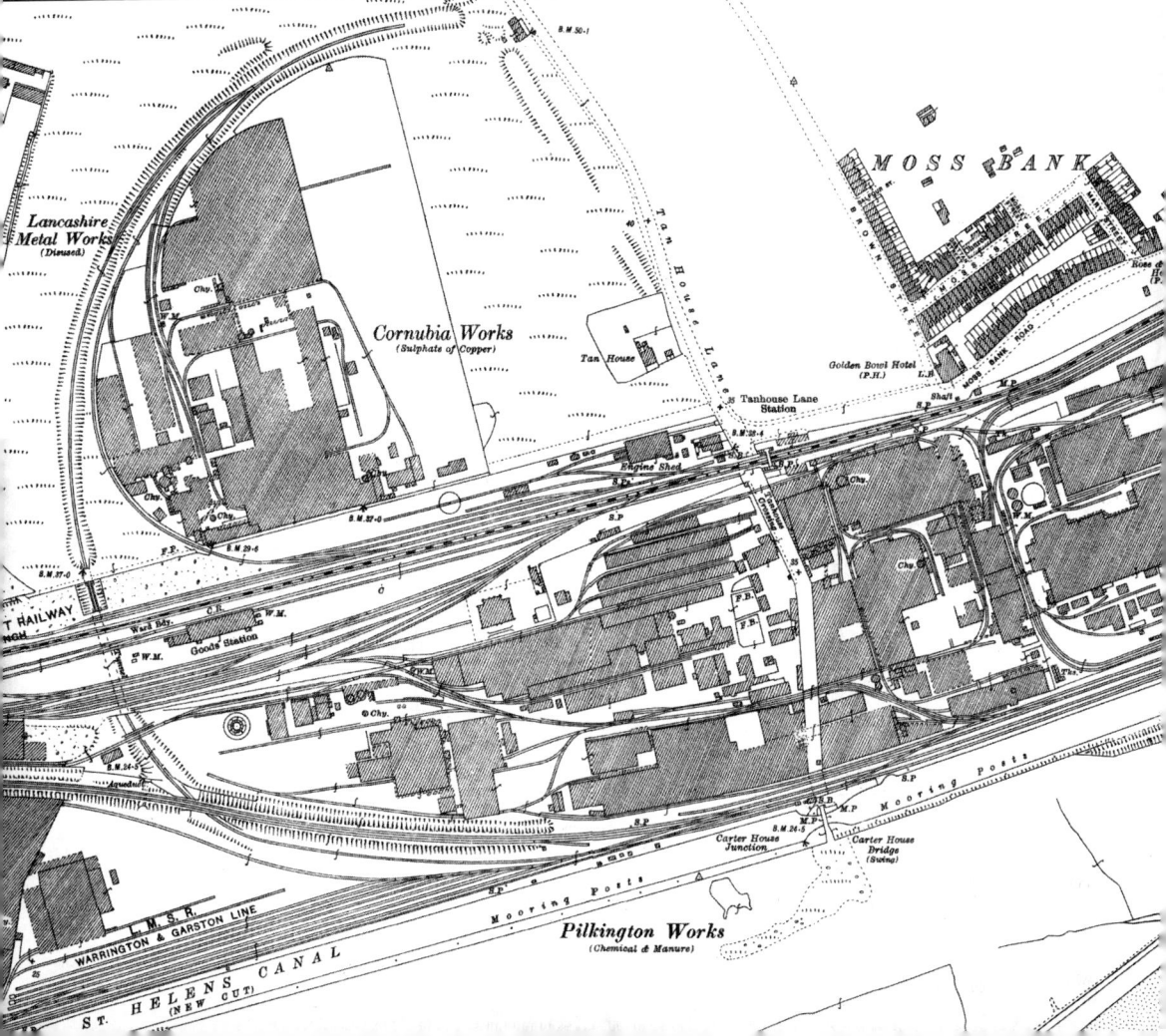

115. The S&M built a two-road loco shed just west of the station on the north side of the line. 3F 0-6-0T no. 7464 was on the allocation between 1935-41 and was photographed on 16th June 1939. It was the only LMS loco based there alongside a handful of LNE shunters. The shed, a sub-shed of Brunswick, closed in 1956. (R.J. Buckley/Initial Photographics)

116. This westward view from 1961 showed two similar platform structures which served throughout the station's life. The footbridge doubled as a right of way when the level crossing was closed to road users. The signal box served until the line's closure; with magnification it could be seen it had at some point been raised on a plinth to improve the signalman's view. The loco shed was behind the station house. (R. Humm coll.)

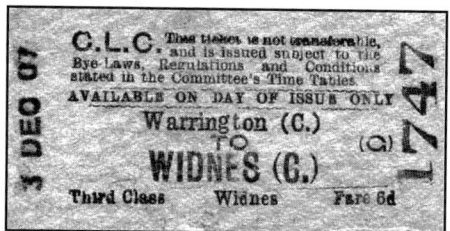

117. Not long before closure 4MT 2-6-0 no. 43010 of Heaton Mersey was seen arriving with a Stockport Tiviot Dale – Liverpool Central service. ICI & Pilkington's Sullivan Works filled the background, including two sidings behind the down platform. (G. Howarth/Disused railways.com)

118. Sometime between June and November 1964, 9F 2-10-0 no. 92019 of Carlisle Kingmoor was recorded leaving Tanhouse Lane goods yard with empty hoppers. These conveyed anhydrite from a quarry at Long Meg, Cumberland, from which sulphur was extracted to make sulphuric acid at the factory of the United Sulphuric Acid Corp, which succeeded the Cornubia Works. This was in production from 1955-73. One of its by-products was slag that was used to make cement. When the factory closed, Blue Circle Ltd continued distribution using cement railed in from Hope, Derbyshire. Following the closure of the Widnes Central loop all traffic for Tanhouse Lane was worked via a link, which the train is just joining, that opened on 16th March 1961, from the Ann Street – Appleton section of the former SH&RG. From 18th April 1982 this was the last part of the SH&RG to close, and a new connection was made from the ex-LNW Widnes Deviation line to serve the Tanhouse Lane terminal, last used by rail traffic in 2000. (See also *Liverpool to Runcorn*.) (E. Bellass/8D Association)

WIDNES CENTRAL

→ 119. Seen in 1948 was a typical contemporary train en route to Liverpool Central. No. 2321 was one of 40 GC class 11B 4-4-0s built between 1901-04 and reclassified to D9 by the LNE. Its Great Central number was 1037, becoming no. 6037 in 1923 until its final change of identity under the LNE's 1947 renumbering scheme. The last D9 was withdrawn in 1950. (Disused-stations.org.uk)

XXX. Widnes Central was 1 mile from Tanhouse Lane. The Widnes Central loop ran in close proximity to the LNW Widnes Deviation (see *Liverpool to Runcorn*) but the two were never physically linked.

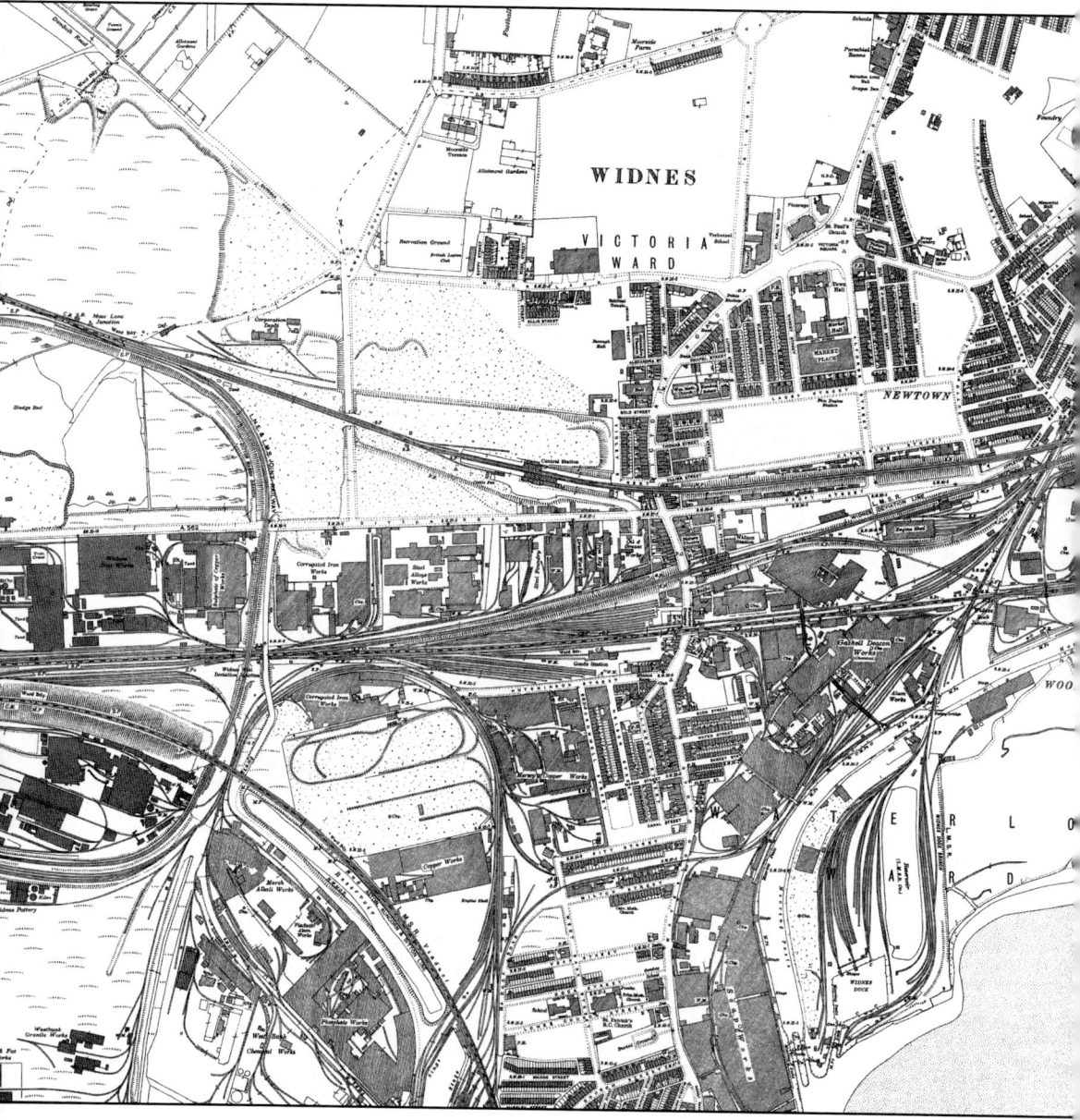

← 120. This was the last up train to call at Widnes Central, the 4.56pm (SO) Liverpool Central – Stockport Tiviot Dale on 3rd October 1964, hauled by an Ivatt 4MT 2-6-0 believed to be no. 43013. There was no direct exit to the street from the up platform, passengers had to use the subway to the opposite side. (Disused-stations.org.uk)

→ Taken around the time of closure this was the exterior of the down side, the main entrance/exit. Note the half-timbered buildings, unusual for a railway station, also the stone setts leading down to Victoria Road, where a right turn would bring a traveller to the entrance to the former LNW Widnes station, until it closed in 1962 (see Liverpool to Runcorn). (D. Nicholas/Disused-stations.org.uk)

West of Widnes Central

At Moor Lane Junction the Ditton Marsh goods branch trailed in. This served the Widnes West Bank Dock Estate and industries at Ditton Marsh on the south side of the LNW Liverpool – Runcorn line. The branch closed from 28th August 1960 and its traffic was diverted to the connection with the SHCR at Hutchinson Street. There was also a goods line with a facing junction with the Widnes Central loop, called the Landowners' Branch, to Ditton. This accessed industries on the north side of the LNW line at Ditton Junction, see map XIV in *Liverpool to Runcorn*.

The Widnes West Railway had a short tunnel at Liverpool Road. The distance from Widnes Central to Hough Green was 2 miles.

EVOLVING THE
Vic Mitchell and Keith Smith
ULTIMATE RAIL ENCYCLOPEDIA
INTERNATIONAL

126a Camelsdale Road, GU27 3RJ. Tel:01730 813169
A-978 0 906520 B- 978 1 873793 C- 978 1 901706 D-978 1 904474
E - 978 1 906008 F - 978 1 908174 G - 978 1 910356

Our RAILWAY titles are listed below. Please check availability by looking at our website **www.middletonpress.co.uk**, telephoning us or by requesting a Brochure which includes our LATEST RAILWAY TITLES also our TRAMWAY, TROLLEYBUS, MILITARY and COASTAL series.

email:info@middletonpress.co.uk

A
Abergavenny to Merthyr C 91 8
Abertillery & Ebbw Vale Lines D 84 5
Aberystwyth to Carmarthen E 90 1
Alnmouth to Berwick G 50 0
Alton - Branch Lines to A 11 6
Ambergate to Buxton G 28 9
Ambergate to Mansfield G 39 5
Andover to Southampton A 82 6
Ascot - Branch Lines around A 64 2
Ashburton - Branch Line to B 95 4
Ashford - Steam to Eurostar B 67 1
Ashford to Dover A 48 2
Austrian Narrow Gauge D 04 3
Avonmouth - BL around D 42 5
Aylesbury to Rugby D 91 3

B
Baker Street to Uxbridge D 90 6
Bala to Llandudno E 87 1
Banbury to Birmingham D 27 2
Banbury to Cheltenham E 63 5
Bangor to Holyhead F 01 7
Bangor to Portmadoc E 72 7
Barking to Southend C 80 2
Barmouth to Pwllheli E 53 6
Barry - Branch Lines around D 50 0
Bartlow - Branch Lines to F 27 7
Basingstoke to Salisbury A 89 4
Bath Green Park to Bristol C 36 9
Bath to Evercreech Junction A 60 4
Beamish 40 years on rails E94 9
Beattock to Carstairs G 84 5
Bedford to Wellingborough D 31 9
Berwick to Drem F 64 2
Berwick to St. Boswells F 75 8
B'ham to Tamworth & Nuneaton F 63 5
Birkenhead to West Kirby F 61 1
Birmingham to Wolverhampton E253
Blackburn to Hellifield F 95 6
Blackburn to Skipton G 85 2
Bletchley to Cambridge D 94 4
Bletchley to Rugby E 07 9
Bodmin - Branch Lines around B 83 1
Bolton to Preston G 61 6
Boston to Lincoln F 80 2
Bournemouth to Evercreech Jn A 46 8
Bradshaw's History F18 5
Bradshaw's Rail Times 1850 F 13 0
Branch Lines series - see town names
Brecon to Neath D 43 2
Brecon to Newport D 16 6
Brecon to Newtown E 06 2
Brighton to Eastbourne A 16 1
Brighton to Worthing A 03 1
Bristol to Taunton D 03 6
Bromley South to Rochester B 23 7
Bromsgrove to Birmingham D 87 6
Bromsgrove to Gloucester D 73 9
Broxbourne to Cambridge F16 1
Brunel - A railtour D 74 6
Bude - Branch Line to B 29 9
Burnham to Evercreech Jn B 68 0
Buxton to Stockport G 32 6

C
Cambridge to Ely D 55 5
Canterbury - BLs around B 58 9
Cardiff to Dowlais (Cae Harris) E 47 5
Cardiff to Pontypridd E 95 6
Cardiff to Swansea E 42 0
Carlisle to Beattock G 69 2
Carlisle to Hawick E 85 7
Carmarthen to Fishguard E 66 6
Caterham & Tattenham Corner B251
Central & Southern Spain NG E 91 8
Chard and Yeovil - BLs a C 30 7
Charing Cross to Orpington A 96 3
Cheddar - Branch Line to B 90 9
Cheltenham to Andover C 43 7
Cheltenham to Redditch D 81 4
Chesterfield to Lincoln G 21 0
Chester to Birkenhead F 21 5
Chester to Manchester F 51 2
Chester to Rhyl E 93 2
Chester to Warrington F 40 6
Chichester to Portsmouth A 14 7
Clacton and Walton - BLs to F 04 8
Clapham Jn to Beckenham Jn B 36 7
Cleobury Mortimer - BLs a E 18 5
Clevedon & Portishead - BLs to D180
Consett to South Shields E 57 4
Cornwall Narrow Gauge D 56 2
Corris and Vale of Rheidol E 65 9
Coventry to Leicester G 00 5
Craven Arms to Llandeilo E 35 2
Craven Arms to Wellington E 33 8
Crawley to Littlehampton A 34 5
Crewe to Manchester F 57 4
Crewe to Wigan G 12 8
Cromer - Branch Lines around C 26 0
Cromford and High Peak G 35 7
Croydon to East Grinstead B 48 0
Crystal Palace & Catford Loop B 87 1
Cyprus Narrow Gauge E 13 0

D
Darjeeling Revisited F 09 3
Darlington Leamside Newcastle E 28 4
Darlington to Newcastle D 98 2
Dartford to Sittingbourne B 34 3
Denbigh - Branch Lines around F 32 1
Derby to Chesterfield G 11 1
Derby to Nottingham G 45 6
Derby to Stoke-on-Trent F 93 2
Derwent Valley - BL to the D 06 7
Devon Narrow Gauge E 09 3
Didcot to Banbury D 02 9
Didcot to Swindon C 84 0
Didcot to Winchester C 13 0
Diss to Norwich G 22 7
Dorset & Somerset NG D 76 0
Douglas - Laxey - Ramsey E 75 8
Douglas to Peel C 88 8
Douglas to Port Erin C 55 0
Douglas to Ramsey D 39 5
Dover to Ramsgate A 78 9
Drem to Edinburgh G 06 7
Dublin Northwards in 1950s E 31 4
Dunstable - Branch Lines to E 27 7

E
Ealing to Slough C 42 0
Eastbourne to Hastings A 27 7
East Croydon to Three Bridges A 53 6
Eastern Spain Narrow Gauge E 56 7
East Grinstead - BLs to A 07 9
East Kent Light Railway A 61 1
East London - Branch Lines of C 44 4
East London Line B 80 0
East of Norwich - Branch Lines E 69 7
Effingham Junction - BLs a A 74 1
Ely to Norwich C 90 1
Enfield Town & Palace Gates D 32 6
Epsom to Horsham A 30 7
Eritrean Narrow Gauge E 38 3
Euston to Harrow & Wealdstone C 89 5
Exeter to Barnstaple B 15 2
Exeter to Newton Abbot C 49 9
Exeter to Tavistock B 69 5
Exmouth - Branch Lines to B 00 8

F
Fairford - Branch Line to A 52 9
Falmouth, Helston & St. Ives C 74 1
Fareham to Salisbury A 67 3
Faversham to Dover B 05 3
Felixstowe & Aldeburgh - BL to D 20 3
Fenchurch Street to Barking C 20 8
Festiniog - 50 yrs of enterprise C 83 3
Festiniog 1946-55 E 01 7
Festiniog in the Fifties B 68 8
Festiniog in the Sixties B 91 6
Ffestiniog in Colour 1955-82 F 25 3
Finsbury Park to Alexandra Pal C 02 8
French Metre Gauge Survivors F 88 8
Frome to Bristol B 77 0

G
Gainsborough to Sheffield G 17 3
Galashiels to Edinburgh F 52 9
Gloucester to Bristol D 35 7
Gloucester to Cardiff D 66 1
Gosport - Branch Lines around A 36 9
Greece Narrow Gauge D 72 2
Guildford to Redhill A 63 5

H
Hampshire Narrow Gauge D 36 4
Harrow to Watford D 14 2
Harwich & Hadleigh - BLs to F 02 4
Harz Revisited F 62 8
Hastings to Ashford A 37 6
Hawick to Galashiels F 36 9
Hawkhurst - Branch Line to A 66 6
Hayling - Branch Line to A 12 3
Hay-on-Wye - BL around D 92 0
Haywards Heath to Seaford A 28 4
Hemel Hempstead - BLs to D 88 3
Henley, Windsor & Marlow - BLa C77 2
Hereford to Newport D 54 8
Hertford & Hatfield - BLs a E 58 1
Hertford Loop E 71 0
Hexham to Carlisle D 75 3
Hexham to Hawick F 08 6
Hitchin to Peterborough D 07 4
Horsham - Branch Lines to A 02 4
Hull, Hornsea and Withernsea G 27 2
Hull to Scarborough G 60 9
Huntingdon - Branch Line to A 93 2

I
Ilford to Shenfield C 97 0
Ilfracombe - Branch Line to B 21 3
Ilkeston to Chesterfield G 26 5
Inverkeithing to Thornton Jct G 76 0
Ipswich to Diss F 81 9
Ipswich to Saxmundham C 41 3
Isle of Man Railway Journey F 94 9
Isle of Wight Lines - 50 yrs C 12 3
Italy Narrow Gauge F 17 8

K
Kent Narrow Gauge C 45 1
Kettering to Nottingham F 82-6
Kidderminster to Shrewsbury E 10 9
Kingsbridge - Branch Line to C 98 7
Kings Cross to Potters Bar E 62 8
King's Lynn to Hunstanton F 58 1
Kingston & Hounslow Loops A 83 3
Kingswear - Branch Line to C 17 8

L
Lambourn - Branch Line to C 70 3
Lancaster to Oxenholme G 77 7
Launceston & Princetown - BLs C 19 2
Leeds to Selby G 47 0
Leek - Branch Line From G 01 2
Leicester to Burton F 85 7
Leicester to Nottingham G 15 9
Lewisham to Dartford A 92 5
Lincoln to Cleethorpes F 56 7
Lincoln to Doncaster G 03 6
Lines around Newmarket G 54 8
Lines around Stamford F 98 7
Lines around Wimbledon B 75 6
Lines North of Stoke G 29 6
Liverpool to Runcorn G 72 2
Liverpool Street to Chingford D 01 2
Liverpool Street to Ilford C 34 5
Llandeilo to Swansea E 46 8
London Bridge to Addiscombe B 20 6
London Bridge to East Croydon A 58 1
Longmoor - Branch Lines to A 41 3
Looe - Branch Line to C 22 2
Loughborough to Ilkeston G 24 1
Loughborough to Nottingham F 68 0
Lowestoft - BLs around E 40 6
Ludlow to Hereford E 14 7
Lydney - Branch Lines around E 26 0
Lyme Regis - Branch Line to A 45 1
Lynton - Branch Line to B 04 6

M
Machynlleth to Barmouth E 54 3
Maesteg and Tondu Lines F 06 2
Majorca & Corsica Narrow Gauge F 41 3
Manchester to Bacup G 46 3
Manchester to Liverpool G 88 3
Mansfield to Doncaster G 23 4
March - Branch Lines around B 09 1
Market Drayton - BLs around F 67 3
Market Harborough to Newark F 86 4
Marylebone to Rickmansworth D 49 4
Melton Constable to Yarmouth Bch E031
Midhurst - Branch Lines of E 78 9
Midhurst - Branch Lines to F 00 0
Minehead - Branch Line to A 80 2
Monmouth - Branch Lines to E 20 8
Monmouthshire Eastern Valleys D 71 5
Moretonhampstead - BL to C 27 7
Moreton-in-Marsh to Worcester D 26 5
Morpeth to Bellingham F 87 1
Mountain Ash to Neath D 80 7

N
Newark to Doncaster F 78 9
Newbury to Westbury C 66 6
Newcastle to Alnmouth G 36 4
Newcastle to Hexham D 69 2
Newmarket to Haughley & Laxfield G 71 5
New Mills to Sheffield G 44 9
Newport (IOW) - Branch Lines to A 26 0
Newquay - Branch Lines to C 71 0
Newton Abbot to Plymouth C 60 4
Newtown to Aberystwyth E 41 3
Northampton to Peterborough F 92 5
North East German NG D 44 9
Northern Alpine Narrow Gauge F 37 6
Northern Spain Narrow Gauge E 83 3
North London Line B 94 7
North of Birmingham F 55 0
North of Grimsby - Branch Lines G 09 8
North Woolwich - BLs around C 65 9
Nottingham to Boston F 70 3
Nottingham to Kirkby Bentinck G 38 8
Nottingham to Lincoln F 43 7
Nottingham to Mansfield G 52 4
Nuneaton to Loughborough G 08 1

O
Ongar - Branch Line to E 05 5
Orpington to Tonbridge B 03 9
Oswestry - Branch Lines around E 60 4
Oswestry to Whitchurch E 81 9
Oxford to Bletchley D 57 9
Oxford to Moreton-in-Marsh D 15 9

P
Paddington to Ealing C 37 6
Paddington to Princes Risborough C819
Padstow - Branch Line to B 54 1
Peebles Loop G 19 7
Pembroke and Cardigan - BLs to F 29 1
Peterborough to Kings Lynn E 32 1
Peterborough to Lincoln F 89 5
Peterborough to Newark F 72 7
Plymouth - BLs around B 98 5
Plymouth to St. Austell C 63 5
Pontypool to Mountain Ash D 65 4
Pontypridd to Merthyr F 14 7
Pontypridd to Port Talbot E 86 4
Porthmadog 1954-94 - BLa B 31 2
Portmadoc 1923-46 - BLa B 13 8
Portsmouth to Southampton A 31 4
Portugal Narrow Gauge E 67 3
Potters Bar to Cambridge D 70 8
Preston & Lancaster - BLs around G 82 1
Preston to Blackpool G 16 6
Preston to the Fylde Coast G 81 4
Preston to Lancaster G 74 6
Princes Risborough - BL to D 05 0
Princes Risborough to Banbury C 85 7

R
Railways to Victory C 16 1
Reading to Basingstoke B 27 5
Reading to Didcot C 79 6
Reading to Guildford A 47 5
Redhill to Ashford A 73 4
Return to Blaenau 1970-82 C 64 2
Rhyl to Bangor F 15 4
Rhymney & New Tredegar Lines E 48 2
Rickmansworth to Aylesbury D 61 6
Romania & Bulgaria NG E 23 9
Ross-on-Wye - BLs around E 30 7
Ruabon to Barmouth E 84 0
Rugby to Birmingham E 37 6
Rugby to Loughborough F 12 3
Rugby to Stafford F 07 9
Rugeley to Stoke-on-Trent F 90 1
Ryde to Ventnor A 19 2

S
Salisbury to Westbury B 39 8
Salisbury to Yeovil B 06 0
Sardinia and Sicily Narrow Gauge F 50 5
Saxmundham to Yarmouth C 69 7
Saxony & Baltic Germany Revisited F 71 0
Saxony Narrow Gauge D 47 0
Scunthorpe to Doncaster G 34 0
Seaton & Sidmouth - BLs to A 95 6
Selsey - Branch Line to A 04 8
Sheerness - Branch Line to B 16 2
Sheffield towards Manchester G 18 0
Shenfield to Ipswich E 96 3
Shildon to Stockton G 79 1
Shrewsbury - Branch Line to A 86 4
Shrewsbury to Chester E 70 3
Shrewsbury to Crewe F 48 2
Shrewsbury to Ludlow E 21 5
Shrewsbury to Newtown E 29 1
Sirhowy Valley Line E 12 3
Sittingbourne to Ramsgate A 90 1
Skegness & Mablethorpe - BL to F 84 0
Slough to Newbury C 56 7
South African Two-foot gauge E 51 2
Southampton to Bournemouth A 42 0
Southend & Southminster BLs E 76 5
Southern Alpine Narrow Gauge F 22 2
South London Line B 46 6
South Lynn to Norwich City F 03 1
Southwold - Branch Line to A 15 4
Spalding - Branch Lines around E 52 9
Spalding to Grimsby F 65 9 6
Stafford to Chester F 34 5
Stafford to Wellington F 59 8
St Albans to Bedford D 08 1
St. Austell to Penzance C 67 3
St. Boswell to Berwick F 44 4
Stourbridge to Wolverhampton E 16 1
St. Pancras to Barking D 68 5
St. Pancras to Folkestone E 88 8
St. Pancras to St. Albans C 78 9
Stratford to Cheshunt F 53 6
Stratford-u-Avon to Birmingham D 77
Stratford-u-Avon to Cheltenham C 25 3
Sudbury - Branch Lines to F 19 2
Surrey Narrow Gauge C 87 1
Sussex Narrow Gauge C 68 0
Swaffham - Branch Lines around F 97
Swanage to 1999 - BL to A 33 8
Swanley to Ashford B 45 9
Swansea - Branch Lines around F 38 3
Swansea to Carmarthen E 59 8
Swindon to Bristol C 96 3
Swindon to Gloucester D 46 3
Swindon to Newport D 30 2
Swiss Narrow Gauge C 94 9

T
Talyllyn 60 E 98 7
Tamworth to Derby F 76 5
Taunton to Barnstaple B 60 2
Taunton to Exeter C 82 6
Taunton to Minehead F 39 0
Tavistock to Plymouth B 88 6
Tenterden - Branch Line to A 21 5
Three Bridges to Brighton A 35 2
Tilbury Loop C 86 4
Tiverton - BLs around C 62 8
Tivetshall to Beccles D 41 8
Tonbridge to Hastings A 44 4
Torrington - Branch Lines to B 37 4
Tourist Railways of France G 04 3
Towcester - BLs around E 39 0
Tunbridge Wells BLs A 32 1

U
Upwell - Branch Line to B 64 0
Uttoxeter to Macclesfield G 05 0
Uttoxetor to Buxton G 33 3

V
Victoria to Bromley South A 98 7
Victoria to East Croydon A 40 6
Vivarais Revisited E 08 6

W
Walsall Routes F 45 1
Wantage - Branch Line to D 25 8
Wareham to Swanage 50 yrs D 09 8
Watercress Line G 75 3
Waterloo to Windsor A 54 3
Waterloo to Woking A 38 3
Watford to Leighton Buzzard D 45 6
Wellingborough to Leicester F 73 4
Welshpool to Llanfair E 49 9
Wenford Bridge to Fowey C 09 3
Wennington to Morecambe G 58 6
Westbury to Bath B 55 8
Westbury to Taunton C 76 5
West Cornwall Mineral Rlys D 48 7
West Croydon to Epsom B 08 4
West German Narrow Gauge D 93 7
West London - BLs of C 50 5
West London Line B 84 8
West Somerset Railway G 78 4
West Wiltshire - BLs of D 12 8
Weymouth - BLs A 65 9
Willesden Jn to Richmond B 71 8
Wimbledon to Beckenham C 58 1
Wimbledon to Epsom B 62 6
Wimborne - BLs around A 97 0
Wirksworth - Branch Lines to G 10 4
Wisbech - BLs around C 01 7
Witham & Kelvedon - BLs a E 82 6
Woking to Alton A 59 8
Woking to Portsmouth A 25 3
Woking to Southampton A 55 0
Wolverhampton to Shrewsbury E 44 4
Wolverhampton to Stafford F 79 6
Worcester to Birmingham D 97 5
Worcester to Hereford D 38 8
Worthing to Chichester A 06 2
Wrexham to New Brighton F 47 5
Wroxham - BLs around F 31 4

Y
Yeovil - 50 yrs change C 38 3
Yeovil to Dorchester A 76 5
Yeovil to Exeter A 91 8
York to Scarborough F 23 9